T0195896

OTHER BOOKS BY THE AUTHOR

The following titles are books by the author

*Fresh Anointing
*From Tears to Cheers
* Don't Give Up!
*Being an Uncommon Achiever
*Destined for Victory
*Fishing for Fruitfulness
*Candidate for the Throne
*Divine Enthronement
*Movement to the Next Level
*Sexual Crimes
*The Key to a Happy Home
*Changing You Story with You Act
*Conquest over Frustration
*7 Habits of Highly Ineffectual People
*Changing Your Darkness to Daystars
*Understanding the Four Phases of Life
*The Potency of Your Word
*The Race, the Rehearsals, the Ring

THE MILLIONAIRE CAPSULE

JOHNSON F. ODESOLA

authorHOUSE®

AuthorHouse™
1663 Liberty Drive
Bloomington, IN 47403
www.authorhouse.com
Phone: 1 (800) 839-8640

Published by AuthorHouse 12/19/2019

ISBN: 978-1-7283-4053-1 (sc)
ISBN: 978-1-7283-4054-8 (e)

Print information available on the last page.

This book is printed on acid-free paper.

Scripture taken from The Holy Bible, King James Version. Public Domain

CONTENTS

ACKNOWLEDGEMENT

All praise to God the Father, Jesus my Savior and the Holy Spirit the director of my life and inspiration. My sincere appreciation to Bisi my wife for her unflinching support and encouragement and to my home church members, Titi, Uche and Enoch. And my special thanks to my spiritual parents Daddy and Mummy E. A. Adeboye they are both my coaches to walk with the Maker of millionaires.

Thank you all may God bless you.

YOUR STOCK CERTIFICATE

This certifies that you are willing to own 1,000,000,000 (One Million) shares of STOCK IN YOURSELF.

This is your certificate of confidence in yourself and your effort, besides, it is your covenant with us to begin right away to use the secrets of making money and avoiding being 'broke' all the time – the secret pioneered by great money makers of the world today – to improve your life for the better and get whatever you desire in your life.

Signature

PROLOGUE

Are you willing to make a lot of money legitimately? But perhaps like many others, you are stuck, not knowing how to?

Maybe you have a job that barely pays enough for you to get through life comfortably. You live from hand to mouth. Pay day to pay day. Ever on the edge!

Or you are an unemployed mother or father of three or four – living in some big city of hustling and bubbling like Lagos, Lusaka and the like. Your whole world can be summed up in a few letters W-O-R-R-I-E-R.

Whatever the case, you need to find ways and means of making a decent, honest living very quickly, as soon as possible.

The business ideas presented in this book are not "get rich quick" schemes. If that is what you want stop the reading immediately. We would not want to lie to you that line of getting riches is easy. It may also attract some legal and moral issues. You will need to work very hard and smart in order to succeed at any of them. You are endowed with the human potentialities that will turn your dreams/vision into reality.

With this book in your hand, you have already embarked on your thousand kilometers journey, now made shorter by this first step. Go for the height!

CHAPTER 1

LIVING IN THE ACTUAL WORLD

Your latest bill has just arrived through the post office. It is red in color and threatening. You have delayed payment. You are being warned that if you do not pay it within seven days, steps will be taken to repossess.

The loan you took to take the family to South Africa or Livingstone falls for holiday is due for servicing. Alimony occasioned by a previous marriage is also overdue. Since this is another month, school fees for the children need to be assembled. Your eldest, Seventeen- year-old daughter Rachel needs a cell phone (all her friends have one) and you must find the money to buy it soonest. To cap it all, your net income is nowhere near equal to your financial obligations. You earn far less than your wants and needs.

There is more awful news. You were brought up to look for a job only for income. You know nothing about earning extra income from other sources. You have wrongly assumed or been misinformed that you must have a massive capital to start any kind of business.

Your world is caving in fast. You cannot sleep at night. You are moody lately. You are stressed and depressed. The whole world is against you. So, as a perfect normal and intelligent person, what do you do next? Start worrying, worrying and worrying yourself near death, but that would not solve the problem.

Think and Start where you are. So what do most people around the world have in common? They all have bills they cannot afford to pay and worry themselves near death about it. Somehow they think by worrying about unsolved problems, the problems will simply go away. Hoping that one morning they will wake up and all their financial problems will disappear into thin air. The truth is you cannot worry away problems.

The real world does not quite work like that. The real world is practical even if luck rained in your direction and you won a charity or lottery it is no guarantee to success. Lottery millionaires tend to overspend, overindulge and since they did not really sweat for their fortune, they have no reason to respect it. Sooner than later, it withers away.

If you sow worry, inactivity, laziness, inertial and complacency, you reap exactly that. But on the other hand, if your sow creativity, thought, hard-work, dedication, adventure and ambition, you will harvest plenty.

Whereas it is only natural to worry about a problem, the smart thing to do is to find a solution (not an answer) to it. An answer is temporary but a solution is permanent. If you have a leaking roof, the answer is to place a container underneath so that the water can drip into it, while the solution, however, would be to seal the hole in the roof.

If you frequently get tired without even doing any heavy work, the answer is to swallow some energy boosting tablets. The solution is to embark on an exercise regime and follow the right diet.

I used to have a teacher who kept pounding away at the class, think and use your brains and minds! Now this is the crest of the matter. Solutions always lie in the art and process of thought. If you think positively and long enough about a particular problem, you will always find a solution (not an answer) to it.

Sir William Hamilton was right when he proclaimed that "On earth, there is nothing great, but man, in man, there is nothing great than mind" Failure is in your mind. Fortune is also in your mind! "As a man thinketh so is he".

Richard Devos said: "The only thing that stands between a man and what he wants from life is often merely the will to try it and the faith to believe that it is possible".

A story was told about a certain gentleman who suffered a lot under the regime of Prime Minister Margaret Thatcher of Great Britain. Some foreigners including him were given by the Thatcher government a 24 hours' notice to vacate the country.

Thatcher had declared the morning following her election to power that Britain was being swamped by foreigners. Soon he would soon be a victim of this school of thought.

Although he had considerable investment in that great country, he was not allowed (by the home office) to dispose of some of his auxiliaries. He found himself penniless and in dire straits

– facing a very uncertain future. He had a child and wife to look after. But guess what; by merely deciding to concentrate (through the art of thought) on finding a solution, he saw light at the end of the very dark tunnel.

He somehow managed to take his young family to that so-called great country, America

Soon after arriving and with a very cooperative wife, he emptied the whole of himself in the street of New York City and hawked bakers ware to keep his body and soul together and devoted the best of his energies into writing. He wrote early in the morning and late at nights in between hawking bakers' ware. Some rubbish it, some mercifully turned into best sellers.

Slowly but surely, he started turning things around for the better. Do not worry-think instead. Think positive.

Think Big And Become A Millionaire!

Listen to Dick Butler as you prepare to become one of the millionaires: "Life isn't fair! It isn't going to be fair! Stop wishing and whining and go out to make it happen for you" It was Horace Walpole who wrote many years ago: "This world is a comedy to those who think but a tragedy to those that feel" Don't be moved by what you feel, hear or read! The way you see things affect the way things go! Remember what Clement Stone said "There is little difference in people, but that little difference makes a big difference. The little difference is attitude. The little difference is whether it is positive or negative" Know that all the water in the world would not be able to sink your boat if it does not get inside of you. Roger Babson: "If things go wrong do not go wrong with them"

Reasons Most People Will Never Get Rich and How To Make Sure You Do

After reading famous self-billionaires one after another I realized many of secrets that make them rich while others continue to struggle.

When you understand and do what self-billionaires do, you get to become one of them. If you don't understand and do what they do you don't get to become one. It's really that simply.

Reasons Most People Will Get Rich

Reason #1 – Waiting to Start

Most people don't want to wait for success. But, at the same time, they are willing to wait before getting started on the road to success.

Do you see the problem here?

The longer you wait to get started, the longer it will be before you get the money, success, and lifestyle you want.

Many people are waiting for everything to be perfect before they get going. Therefore, they never get going and never get the rewards.

No race has ever been won (or even finished) by someone who never left the starting line. Don't wait to get going. Start today on the road to success.

Reason #2- Being Financially Illiterate

The cornerstone of all wealth 'understands the difference between assets and liabilities'.

The difference is this: Assets put money IN your pocket; liabilities take money OUT of your pocket.

Most people thing their home, car, and other possessions are assets.

But, the truth is that in most cases those things take money out of your pocket. They COST you money. They don't MAKE you money.

Therefore, by the true definition above, those things are liabilities. They take money OUT of your pocket each month. When you have more money coming IN from real assets than you have going OUT to pay for liabilities, you will be financially free.

Reason #3 – Not Understanding or Using Systems for Making Money

A system for making money is anything that allows you to make money without your own effort. In other words, it's automated way money.

All true assets are simply "systems" of one sort or another.

Once you create or invest in a proven system for making money, there is no limit to the money you can make.

Becoming a master of money system can bring you riches beyond your dreams.

Reason 4# - Not Being Persistent or Patient Enough

To finish any race you have to leave the starting line and follow though the finish line. Most people create their failure by either not getting started or not following though, or both. To get rich, successful, and happy you must have the patience and persistence to cross the finish line. You must not only get started, but also follow through.

This may sound obvious, but it's still the cause of most failure.

Only by joining the small percentage of people who are willing to do the things mentioned above will you have the greatest chances for wealth and success. It's really quite simple…Decide to do these things and you can get rich too. If you don't do them, then like most people you may never get rich.

Decide now to master the ideas mentioned above and begin your road to success now. Then follow through and watch the difference it makes.

CHAPTER 2

THE 13 MILLIONAIRE LAWS

Here are the secrets of success that heaven is dropping to your life so as to be able to make your mark on the planet earth. When you pick the currency in any country, which is called money, it is just a printed paper representation, that paper is in your wallet on pocket is not the real money. Money is an idea! Your wealth or earning of more money has nothing to do with the kind of job you are doing or the volume of paper or coin you are caring. It has to do with the consciousness. Poverty- consciousness will cause a person to see, hear, smell, think and feel poverty, lack and limitation.

Mike Todd wrote; "Being broke is a temporary situation. Being poor are a mental state". The fact that you even loss money in any business deal does not make you poor! Poverty and prosperity are mental states! Note that all money that you will ever need on this planet earth are all deposited inside of you. You are to work out your prosperity with daily affirmation, diligence and patience.

To prosper more and more:

- Doing whatever you are doing now more effectively.
- Add value! Improving the quality and quantity of the service you render!
- Thinking daily of how you can help humanity in a better way!

- Reject poverty conscience or mentality. That is to say you need to maintain a balance between prosperity with trembling in the fear of God.
- Determine to earn more money! Are you aware that it is the 4% wealthy in any society that controls 96% of all the money that is earned? Here are my researches on the laws that make Millionaires what they are: Get ready to join that group!

The Law of Responsibility

This law states that; "If it is to be, it is up to me"! Nobody is to be blame for your life but you! Take responsibility for your life we are living in a society where people blame everything from their parents to the government for their failure to get ahead in life. Those who succeed in life are men and women who refused to buy into the mentality that says "I could succeed if only it weren't for so and so". They realized that when you say someone or something outside of yourself is preventing you from succeeding, you're giving away your power to that someone or something. You are saying, "You have more control over my life than I do!" Successful people don't buy into this victim thinking. Rather, their personal credo is "I am responsible for all that happens to my life, nobody else"! Adolf Montiel Ballesterous wrote to his boy: "Son you can find on the outside only what you possess on the inside".

If you want automatic change or instant change you are only adding unnecessary frustration. Change is neither automatic nor instant. You can avoid compressed timelines that only create anxiety by realizing that time is on your side if you act now and act consistently. By taking responsibility for your own happiness you place yourself as the real agent of change. Everything else becomes a resource to assist you on your journey and you release yourself from random chance and instead you create your own opportunities and can recognize opportunities that are favorable for helping you achieve your goals. Do not forget that what you believe determines what you become and never forget that the only thing in life achieved without effort is failure. So refuse to stop yourself. No matter what happens around you, push on until you reach your destination.

William Arthur said: "If you can imagine it, you can achieve it. If you can dream it, you can become it".

Resist self-pity and depression. Christopher Morely said: "There are three ingredients in the good life: learning, earning and yearning". But incidentally no one can do any of the three for you except yourself. Continue to learn, never lose your yearning power! Devil wants you to drop your pursuit and hang your harps by the rivers of Babylon. You have not got to your destination! It is not time to stop, until your arrival is celebrated. The state of your life is nothing more than the state of your mind. Build positive thoughts around your life and take responsibility for everything that comes! Adjust where-ever you need to.

No one knows what is in him until he tries and many will never try if they were not forced by circumstances. For this reason Abraham Maslow said: "A musician must make music; an artist must paint. A poet must write if he is to be ultimately at peace with himself. What a man can be, he must be". Never retire! Never resign! Never give up! Take responsibility to become all you can be in life! Determine to be superior to your former self. Take responsibility for your life, when we mess up, we need to fess up, fix it up and move on! Stop blaming! Some of us blame past circumstances for our failure. Big deal! Your childhood may be very depressing and the outlook dim, but you should not let that determine your future. Here is what a wise man says recently, "our background and circumstances may influence who we are, but we are responsible for what we become".

The Law of Visualization

This law states that; only what you see and focus on is your entitlement. In line with this definition you must resist all distraction. Keep a clear focus on where you are going because your success in life will be determined largely by how clear you can see what you really want.

"In order to use creative visualization to create what you want in life, you must be willing and able to accept the best that life has to offer you-- your 'good'." Shakti Gawain

Visualization Is Easy To Use

Like all the other tools of creation, we use visualization every day to create our experience of reality. Daydreaming, fantasizing, mental rehearsals, and imagination are all examples of visualization. We have all daydreamed about an upcoming vacation or a visit with a favorite friend. Many of us have fantasized about winning the lottery or getting a better job. Unfortunately, due to lack of knowledge about the power of our images, we also often use visualization to create experiences we do not want in our lives. We mentally rehearse our greatest fears over and over in our minds.

Have you ever imagined how you would respond if you were robbed or attacked, mentally rehearsed an imagined argument with your co-worker, had a daydream about the death of a loved one, or imagined the worst possible outcome to a situation you were experiencing?

If you answered yes to any of the above questions, you are using the powerful force of mental imagery to create things you do not desire in your life. Although humanity has always used some form of mental imagery, it has only been in the last few years that the power of visualization techniques has been taught widely in our society.

Businesses train their employees to use visualization to improve performance and production. Coaches use visualization with athletes because research has shown that mental rehearsal is an effective way to increase athletic performance. Students use visualization to improve test scores while therapists use imagery to enhance relaxation skills.

Positive Visualization

The two components of an effective positive visualization technique are a clear image of what you want to create combined with a strong positive emotion. Mental images do not always come in the form of a picture. Some people use words, thoughts, or sensations to create a mental image.

The Visualization Process

The first step in doing a positive visualization is determining what you want to create in your life. If you do not know specifically what it is you want to manifest in your life, you can create with "broad brushstrokes."

[For more information, please visit https://law-of-attraction-info.com/power-visualization/]

If you are certain of the specific details you want to manifest, you can clearly imagine these events in your mind's eye. There is nothing wrong with creating something specific; however, manifestation often comes more quickly if you leave the details of your creation to your Higher Self.

For example, you tell me you would like a new car. By itself this does not sound to exciting does it? Well guess what, it's likely not exciting enough to make your subconscious do the things it needs to do to move you towards the goal either. Instead let us try adding a little visualization to the statement instead. See yourself shopping for that new car...its red, or perhaps black. It's the perfect size to take your children to little league or maybe spend a night out with friends. We are driving around town in our new vehicle and having a great time. You see my friend; the key is that with the right amount of visualization applied we allow our minds to see objects as real things that are indeed reachable; then wait for God to surprise you with something better than you could have imagined.

Visualization Can Be Applied To Many Areas and Be Just As Effective

You say you have a meeting with the boss? Try running through the meeting in your mind. Imagine it going extremely well. Above all else make it as real as possible in your mind. Applying visualization techniques can help to subconsciously program ourselves for achievement. Visualization is a powerful tool of consciousness. Combine visualization with prayer, faith, or love to assist you in soaring above any crisis that may come your way.

The Law of Correspondence

This law says that; your outer world is like a mirror that reflects back to you what is going on in your inner world. This powerful law when paraphrased it will read. "As within, so without". One can also explain the law thus. "Everything that happens outsides you corresponds to something that is going on inside of you". You must never forget that your outer world is a reflection of your inner world. A man is what he thinks. Since your world reflects your thought, you must resist all traces of negative thoughts! Marcus Aurelia told his alumni: "Our life is what our thoughts make it". Aristotle also declared to his pen friend: "We are what we repeatedly do". No wonder Margo James told his stepson: "The answer is simple, if you want something very badly, you can achieve it". Focus regularly on what you want to be and where you desire to reach! Resist fear, depression, inferiority, complex, doubt, confusion, immoral thoughts and the likes. What a man thinks of himself, determines his fate. This is because, as within so without and whatever happens outside of you coincides with what is going on inside of you.

The Law of Concentration

It states that energy focused on single pursuit yields better and lasting result. We live in a world of scattered energy and focus. Divided attention will lead to unfounded divided achievement. Vince Lombardi said; Wining is not everything! It is only one thing. No matter your current pain; hold on your focus: William Boetcker said: "The difficulties and struggles of today are the best price we must pay for the accomplishment and victories of tomorrow". Stephen Covey wrote to his daughter; "live out your imagination, not your history". People who succeed do not have fewer problems than people who fail. (As a matter of fact, the only people without problems are those in the cemeteries). It is not what happens to us that separates failures from successes. It is how we perceive it and what we do about what happens that makes the difference! Hold On! Don't forget that thousand died before today! Remember that if you woke up this morning with more health than illness, you are more blessed than the millions who will not survive this week! If you have food in your refrigerator, clothes to wear, a roof over your head and a place to sleep, you are richer than 75% of this world! If you have money in the bank or in your wallet, you are among the top 8% of the world's wealthy ones! If you hold up your head with a smile on your face and truly thankful, you are blessed because the majority can, but most do not! Yes the majority will rather complain rather than comply with praise. Yes the majority will rather murmur than muse over God's goodness.

Take time to enjoy the simple things of life for such is life. Denis Waitley said: "It is not what you are that holds you back. It is what you think you are not". Refuse to confusion and diversion, concentrate on your vision and journey even if you think you are not what you should! Let us mind in the beginning the things that matter in the end! Pray and Plan! Plan and pray! He that fails to plan, plans to fail! Never quit because someone disagrees with you! You've got to knock and knock and knock and knock until you knock it open or you knock it down. But never, never, never give up!

The enemy of success is out to disorganize you and disgrace your destiny! Distraction is used to paralyze many potential giants in the generation gone bye. He distracted Adam and Eve, Moses and the likes. You must not be the next victim! Clarity is anti-distraction agent! It kills deviation, paralyses derailment and quenches indecision! So you must be person of clear vision. Vision enhances focus, it infuses energy, eradicate waste, it produces passion, it gives direction.

Fight distraction daily! Re-writing your goal is a fast way of looking to clarity! Clarity accounts for 80% of success. Lack of clarity is a leading cause of frustration in life and endeavor. Never forget that; "Success is goals and all else is mere complementary! Washington Irving wrote "Great minds have purpose, little minds have wishes", keep your vision and your mind with all diligent, with this you will be able to fight every distraction each day from every angles. St. Theresa of Lisicus did write: "Each small task everyday is part of the total harmony of the universe". Never stop seeing where you are going!

The Law of Affirmation

Affirmations are statements of what you want in your life. Affirmations reflect the spiritual law of perfection everywhere now. They are based on Spiritual Truth not your current experience of life.

Some people have trouble with affirmations because they feel they are not speaking the truth when they use an affirmation. For instance, if you are sick and you say, "I am whole, healthy, and energized," it might feel like a lie; however, affirmations are not the facts of your current situation. They represent the experiences you want to have in your life.

Affirmations are not a method of communication; they are a tool of creation. If you want to tell your neighbor about the facts in your life, do not use an affirmation. But, if you want to create a new reality, use affirmations.

Remember, even your idle words have power. Telling your neighbor the facts of your current problem adds energy to those problems. If your neighbor can not help you, use the power of your words to create what you want, and not what you do not want.

I once heard a story about a farmer who dreamed of having a large herd of cattle. He only had enough money to purchase one cow. This man knew the power of words; so, he named his one cow Herd. The neighbors thought he was crazy to be talking about his herd when they could see only one cow in the field; nevertheless, this farmer talked about his herd every chance he got. As the story goes, his words soon returned to him fulfilled, and he obtained a large herd of cattle. Learn to use the power of affirmations and your life will reflect the new image your words express.

[Visit http://www.free-positive-thought.com/uploads/5/7/0/0/5700463/affirmation.pdf for more information.]

The Law of Desire

You are here to live abundantly and live out your greatest dreams and potential. If you aren't living then you are growing and if you aren't growing then that will lead to an erosion of your passion, desire and happiness. You should resolve in your heart that to live fully free! In other words...liberty and freedom is your only option and anything less than that must be discarded and avoided. Do not allow past performance to cheat and rob you, you are unlimited. I charge you to challenge yourself to become who you must be to obtain the success you want. You will have to surrender old thoughts, old ways and the old luggage of the past. It's a very challenging thing to change our thought patterns and behavior patterns. But you must be fully committed to changing. If your liberty and freedom is tied up on thinking and doing things differently then you must change! Indeed, you have to think and do things differently to get new and different results. Surrender your old self and put on the new self. Choose to be brand new! Choose to press into liberty and challenge yourself to continue growth, change and desire.

The Law of Attraction

The Law says you are a living magnet. "It says that your thought creates a force field of energy that radiates out from you and attracts back to your life people and circumstances in harmony with them". Any thought you have combine with an emotion- positive or negative, radiate out from you and attract back to your life, the people, circumstances, ideas and opportunities consistent with it.

This law is the principle defining the law of sowing and reaping! That means if you have a clear idea in your mind of any desired goal in life on a continual basis, you will inevitably draw into your life the resources that you needed in order to achieve it! Hold continually thoughts and ideas (picture) of good health, wealth, good living, power, purity, greatness, faster progress, better accommodation, car and better family life. Hold continually the picture of progress and joy! Continually see yourself living loins and dedicating your children, picture yourself singing and dancing with your grandchildren around your rocky chain! Continually see yourself having great divine power for this generation!

Refuse to see the lies of the devil and refuse to harbor any thoughts not consistent with what you desire to be.

Mr Hepatis says "the soul is dyed the color of its thoughts. Think only things that are in line with your principles and bear the light of the day.

The content of your character is your choice. Day to day what you think and what you do is who you become ---" It is the law of attraction.

Ways to Attract Abundance and Prosperity

When you hear the words "abundance" and "prosperity", what immediately comes to mind? Is it money, fulfilling relationships, a lovely house to live in, peace of mind, a career/vocation that expresses your gifts? It may be all or none of those things. It may mean something else to you. But if you want to attract more prosperity and abundance into your life, no matter how you define them, then this article outlines 5 key ways to do so.

1. Understand Attraction Law

Another way to look at the Law of Attraction is by looking at the definition of Abraham Hicks, which states that "you attract whatever you give your attention and energy to, whether wanted or unwanted". So, if you're curious about what you're putting out there, look at what you are attracting, the visible results in your life.

Knowing about and working with the Law of Attraction will help you in manifesting, creating and attracting more abundance and prosperity in your life. Once you understand it, there's no turning back.

2. You Get What You Focus On

One of the key concepts in the Law of Attraction is that you get what you focus on, whether that be money, relationships, employment etc). So when you focus on having less, that is the experience you create for yourself. Saying that "I hate my job" will just draw even more attention to the aspects of the job that you don't like. Even if you look for another job, it'll be with that negative energy.

Just wanting something isn't enough, because you will still continue to think about what you don't have. Always focusing on what you lack means that you don't see the present and future opportunities, or begin to realize your true desires. You're getting in your own way!

3. Clear Your Head

This is to allow you to focus more effectively. Our minds are full of "stuff"; old, tired and limiting beliefs, which don't reflect who we are now, or who we want to become. Set aside quiet time for yourself on a regular basis to get real clear about what you really want to attract in your life. Use this opportunity to ask yourself questions.

Ask yourself: "How can I create more prosperity and abundance in my life?". Once your head is clear, you will allow the answers to come to you. Meditation is a great way to start clearing the mind.

4. Appreciate Life's Abundance

Appreciating life's abundance is another way to opening yourself up to accept more abundance and prosperity in your life. When you fully appreciate what you have in your life, the Universe has a way of giving you more. Keep a gratitude journal and at the end of each day, write down everything that you appreciate in your life. You'll begin to change your energy and vibration and become more internally aligned with what you want to create in your life.

5. Use Prosperity Affirmations

As you write your gratitude journal, it is an opportunity to write down prosperity affirmations as well. Affirmations are statements of acceptance that you use to manifest your destiny or what you want to create in your life. They are powerful, positive thoughts and words sent out to the universe.

If you want to use affirmations to create positive changes in your life, then you must first BELIEVE that this is possible. It shouldn't be a halfhearted "well, I'll give this a go and see what happens".

To make affirmations more effective, put as much positive energy in writing and saying them as possible. Visualize what you want to create and let this inform your prosperity affirmations.

When you cease operating from a position of lack, you start to create the fertile conditions to make more informed decisions, identify greater opportunities and attract more abundance and prosperity into your life.

The Law of Positive Approach

If you do not think you have something to offer, why should anyone else? You don't have to wave a banner to sell yourself, but self-deprecation won't do it either. An exercise to do with your support group is to imagine yourself as a product. What's special about you the product? Why would someone want to 'buy' this product? Who are your 'customers'? How will you reach them? Odd questions to ask yourself, but they will put a new slant on looking at yourself more objectively. Then you need to create a Marketing Plan to launch this new product onto the world.

Here are a few questions that may help you uncover you sweet spot. What do you feel you are good at right now?

What do others say about your abilities? In other words, what do others praise you for being able to do well and that they wish they could do it like you?

What is your current expertise or what do you know the most about?

What is your passion pattern? In other words, what do you find yourself doing most frequently with the most passion or what are your frequently passionate interests?

What types of things are you very intuitive about or what activities demonstrate your natural talents (natural brilliance)?

Does your current activity make full use of your natural talents and abilities?

Are you happy with your current work and life? If not, why not? What will make you happy?

Life is full of purpose. You have to find yours. That's right...YOU have to do it. Part of our journey of success is discovering what our purpose is. You should not be frustrated by the fact that you may not know what you want to do or what your purpose may be. While in reality, this can indeed be a frustrating aspect of life...embrace the discovery process and enjoy exploring the possibilities for what you want to and what you want to become.

If you want automatic change or instant change you are only adding unnecessary frustration. Change is neither automatic nor instant. You can avoid compressed timelines that only create anxiety by realizing that time is on your side if you act now and act consistently. By taking responsibility for your own happiness you place yourself as the real agent of change. Everything else becomes a resource to assist you on your journey and you release yourself from random chance and instead you create your own opportunities and can recognize opportunities that are favorable for helping you achieve your goals.

The Law of Reciprocity

The harvest of what you make happen for others will come back to you.

A major part of the process of achieving success and living the kind of life that you dream of is to give. Many people think that to get what you want you have to take it. There is a universal truth though that the true path to get what you want is to give. When you give, you get. What you sow, you shall reap. If this is true, then what is it we must give? Here are my suggestions.

Gives Others Your Honesty

The world we live in has a simple rule that most follow: Lie when you have to. Unfortunately, if this makes other people climb up the ladder, it makes the poor even poorer. Success does not necessarily mean to have money, but success is when you have a great personality and treatment to other people. To be successful, character should not be sacrificed. We shall keep our feet on the ground as we reach every goal.

Give Others Your Respect

We shall never judge a book by its cover. We do not give respect depending on how well that person has done to you. In order to obtain success, we must learn to pay respect to everyone who is due of respect.

Give Others Your Vulnerability

We are taught to "be strong." And yes, we should be strong. But we have also embraced something that I think keeps us from having the kind of life that we long for. No one is ever perfect. It is not necessary to show and tell people you are weak but accept the fact to yourself that you too have a weakness. And this weakness, instead of this to become a hindrance, let that weakness be your inspiration to make yourself better as you climb up the ladder and reach success.

Give Others Your Care

Too many people forget how to care about others. People pass by each other without courtesy and care. Something so essential when reaching once goal. Let us make people feel they are cared about. This would mean to say, you are someone whom can be trusted as what other's feelings always matter to you.

Give Others Your Passion

There is nothing this world needs more than passionate people. And people need passionate people. Hustle is always tiring – life, work, and the balance you want is always tiring. But when passion surrounds you and your eagerness to reach your goal will always and shall always lead you to your expected Finish Line!

Give Others Your Experience

We are all masters of our own experience. Our experiences for sure has taught us how we can live life better and through sharing your experience, you are not just helping other's get through and reach their dreams but you are helping yourself too. Practicing your experience will make you well verse in every aspect you are focusing at.

Give Others Your Help

Zig Ziglar says that if we will "help others get what they want; we will in turn get what we want." If we want to be successful, it is always necessary to lend a helping hand. Not because you expect others to help you too but team work shall bring you to the success you are aiming.

[for more information, please visit http://www.appleseeds.org/7-Things-Success.htm]

The Law of Progression

Do you remember a time when you had a big and lofty visualization? Maybe you wanted to be a star in venture of life, an organ transplant doctor, or a world-class tri-athlete. Perhaps you dreamed of crossing the ocean in a sailboat or chiseling sculpture out of mountain rock. As a youngster, you may have worked hard toward achieving that dream. You talked about it with your every acquaintance and most distant relation whenever you had the opportunity. But slowly you drifted away from your heart's desire. What happened?

The answer is easy: You got distracted! You got confused. Your friends enticed you into joining their parade. You were no longer in rhythm with who you are. The law of momentum in physics says that a body in motion tends to remain in motion until an outside force acts upon it. Distractions by my own opinion is that force. Your friends or family members acted upon you by overly discouraging you, or by encouraging you to follow a more "sensible" path. So you stopped practicing, stopped studying, stopped working toward your highest ambition. All those distractions and "sensible" decisions competed for your attention. Your grand dream gradually became just a footnote in the history of your life.

Have you ever heard the truism that says "used to bees make no honey"? Do you know people who are always talking about what they used to do? They usually say, "Someday I will pick it up again." But that's a weak excuse for avoiding the risk of living your dream. The time is now! When you have a worthy goal—something that is worth going after, you have to apply the law of critical success to your life. This law says that you should always be doing something that moves you closer to your goal. Question: What are you doing today that is drawing you a little bit nearer to accomplishing your dream?

Shakespeare wrote, "This above all, to thine own self be true." Bravo, Mr. Shakespeare! Being true to yourself means that you do what matters most to you, regardless of what else is competing for your time. Our deeds and achievements are the only yardsticks we can use to measure our integrity, and the only evidence we can use to judge whether we have been true to ourselves.

From now on, why not put the law of momentum into action? It is said that motion creates emotion. When you take action toward that which you most desire, your self-confidence will soar. Distractions shift you off-course or slow you down; actions accelerate you forward along your chosen course. Every action strengthens you to take another. You will become unstoppable!

You will liberate yourself from guilt and self-pity. You will become the envy of the world. Many people never commit to anything. They have interests and hobbies, but no passion or driving ambition. I believe that you are one of those people who can commit; otherwise you wouldn't be reading this article.

Life is like a bicycle. The moment we stop pedaling, we start losing momentum. If we coast for too long, we fall. Resolve to press on in spite of all your distractions.

Here is what you can do to get whatever you want in life: First, identify your distractions and move away from them. By doing so, you will become effective rather than merely efficient. Being effective means doing the right things, while being efficient means doing things right. It's nice to be efficient, but it doesn't do you any good if you're not doing the things that will move you toward your dream. Focus first on being effective; let efficiency come as it may.

Second, write the word MOMENTUM in big letters and hang it somewhere that you will see it often. Do something daily that will bring you closer to your goal.

Third, make a public commitment by asking your friends—those who are positive and encouraging—to hold you accountable. Talk about your dream with them to begin edging it into the world. Speak of it as something that you are doing, not something that you think about doing.

Finally, learn all you can about the lore of your passion. If you are not, at the least, more knowledgeable than the average person about the subject of your dream, you are fooling somebody—yourself.

So, my friend, live your finest ambition. Do it because you must. You probably won't find any help when you begin. You will, however, get all the help you want when you are already there. So be true to thine own self. Honesty is the iron string that vibrates within every heart. Let results be the measure of your integrity. Work hard at it. Do more than is expected, more than is common. Keep the momentums going! I wish you incredible success!

The Law of Second Thought

The law says "before you quit one venture get another view from a different angle".

Does it not just burn you up when you have just shared your 'great idea' with someone and not only are they not as enthusiastic as you; they even go as far as to say your idea would not work! If this has happened to you then you are not alone.

In such instances we generally have two choices. One, we can let go of the idea and be left with the dreaded "what if I can only tried" question running through our minds. Or two, we can get a second opinion!

Luckily for us the people from the next few examples did just that!

"Computers in the future may weigh no more than 15 tons." - Popular Mechanics," forecasting the relentless march of science, 1949.

"I think there is a world market for maybe five computers." - Thomas Watson, chairman of

IBM, 1943.

"I have travelled the length and breadth of this country and talked with the best people, and I can assure you that data processing is a fad that won't last out the year." - The editor in charge of business books for Prentice Hall, 1957.

"But what...is it good for?" - Engineer at the Advanced Computing Systems Division of

IBM commenting on the microchip, 1968.

"There is no reason anyone would want a computer in their home." - Ken Olson, president, chairman and founder of Digital Equipment Corp., 1977.

"This 'telephone' has too many shortcomings to be seriously considered as a means of communication. The device is inherently of no value to us." - Western Union internal memo, 1876.

"The wireless music box has no imaginable commercial value. Who would pay for a message sent to nobody in particular?" - David Sarnoff's associates in response to his urgings for investment in the radio in the 1920s.

"The concept is interesting and well-formed, but in order to earn better than a 'C,' the idea must be feasible." - A Yale University management professor in response to Fred Smith's paper proposing reliable overnight delivery service. (Smith went on to found Federal Express Corp.) Who the heck wants to hear actors talk?" - Harry M. Warner, Warner Brothers, 1927.

"I'm just glad it'll be Clark Gable who's falling on his face and not Gary Cooper." - Gary

Cooper on his decision not to take the leading role in "Gone with the Wind."

"A cookie store is a bad idea. Besides, the market research reports say America likes crispy cookies, not soft and chewy cookies like you make." - Response to Debbi Fields' idea of starting her company, Mrs. Fields' Cookies.

"We don't like their sound, and guitar music is on the way out." - Decca Recording Co. rejecting the Beatles, 1962.

"Heavier-than-air flying machines are impossible." - Lord Kelvin, president, Royal Society, 1895.

"If I had thought about it, I wouldn't have done the experiment. The literature was full of examples that said you can't do this." - Spencer Silver on the work that led to the unique adhesives or 3-M "Post-It" Notepads.

"So we went to Atari and said, 'Hey, we've got this amazing thing, even built with some of your parts, and what do you think about funding us? Or we'll give it to you. We just want to do it. Pay our salary; we'll come work for you.' And they said, 'No.' So then we went to Hewlett-Packard, and they said, 'Hey, we don't need you; you haven't got through college yet.'" - Apple Computer Inc. founder Steve Jobs on attempts to get Atari and H-P interested in his and Steve Wozniak's personal computer.

"Professor Goddard does not know the relation between action and reaction and the need to have something better than a vacuum against which to react. He seems to lack the basic knowledge ladled out daily in high schools." - New York Times editorial about Robert Goddard's revolutionary rocket work, 1921.

"You want to have consistent and uniform muscle development across all of your muscles? It can't be done. It's just a fact of life. You just have to accept inconsistent muscle development as an unalterable condition of weight training." -Response to Arthur Jones, who solved the "unsolvable" problem by inventing Nautilus.

"Drill for oil? You mean drill into the ground to try and find oil? You're crazy." - Drillers who Edwin L. Drake tried to enlist to his project to drill for oil in 1859.

Stocks have reached what looks like a permanently high plateau." - Irving Fisher, Professor of Economics, Yale University, 1929.

Airplanes are interesting toys but of no military value." - Mrechal Ferdinand Foch, Professor of Strategy, Ecole Superieure de Guerre.

"Everything that can be invented has been invented." - Charles H. Duell, Commissioner, U.S. Office of Patents, 1899.

"Louis Pasteur's theory of germs is ridiculous fiction". - Pierre Pachet, Professor of Physiology at Toulouse, 1872.

"The abdomen, the chest and the brain will forever be shut from the intrusion of the wise and humane surgeon." - Sir John Eric Ericksen, British surgeon, appointed Surgeon- Extraordinary to Queen Victoria, 1873.

"640k ought to be enough for anybody." - Bill Gates, 1981.

Wow! Can you imagine what would have happened if the folks who heard these "expert opinions" hadn't gone for a second opinion? Never fear following your passion.

The Law of Persistence

"Nothing in this world can take the place of persistence. Talent will not; nothing is more common than unsuccessful people with talent. Genius will not; unrewarded genius is almost a proverb. Education will not; the world is full of educated derelicts. Persistence and determination alone are omnipotent. The slogan 'press on' has solved and always will solve the problems of the human race." Calvin Coolidge

[For more information visit, https://virtuefirst.info/virtues/tenacity/]

Sometimes You Just Have To Outlast The Others

The truth is that a person can only be successful if he masters the ability to absorb, intake and ingest failures. "One more week. Just give it one more week." It could be difficult in the beginning but as time goes by, you will learn to take things one step at a time. Understanding that the next day is another day to strive. It is the will and passion to make yourself better and prove yourself to another person.

Sometimes You Just Have To Hold On To The End

"When you get to the end of your rope, tie a knot and hang on." Franklin Roosevelt

There are many people who has quit on the first try. Many has given up when they feel like they cannot be able make it anymore. But for those who have tried on the tenth time, they show perseverance in never giving up. Self-reliance is the key! Belief in themselves.

Sometimes The Most Beautiful Result Comes From Dull Things Under Pressure

"Diamonds are nothing more than chunks of coal that stuck to their jobs." Malcolm Forbes

Like a diamond, we also have to go through a lot of things and be under pressure so in the end we will shine and shimmer like a diamond as our goals be one step closer to us already. We have to take it in, absorb the difficulty and let it be the foundation of a stronger version of yourself.

[Please visit and read http://www.appleseeds.org/Widener_Tenacity.htm]

Trials will surely come. Life will get hard.

You will want to quit.

Then you will have a choice: Will you give up? Or will you take your turn at tenacious. The choice you make will determine much of the rest of your life.

CHAPTER 3

THE 36 SELF DEFICIENCIES

First, I am enormously relieved to note that you have decided to heed my advice – to stop worrying and start thinking positive and big. This is the only way you can embark on this fascinating journey unburdened. However, you first need to get rid of some negative and poisonous chemicals from your system. All institutionalized and embedded in your mind. Standing in the way of your success. Until your mind is free of these negative chemicals, you won't get very far. So let us start afresh.

NO. 1: Wrong Socialization

You have been wrongly indoctrinated… (You were brought up to look to jobs only for income). We are the way we were brought up. We think, act and behave the way societies shaped us in our formative years.

Because you were brought up to believe that the only way you can get ahead in life is through employment, you have institutionalized this in your mind; to you being employed by someone else seems to be the only way out. However, societies have forged ahead, (Japan and America) they have done so because they subscribe to the spirit of free enterprise and the culture of creativity. These two great countries are the leading economies of the world because they nurtured industrialists such as Ford, Rockefeller, Getty, Hughes, Gates, Toyota, Mitsubishi, Morita and countless others in their societies.

So the way to forge forward is to be innovative and creative. To think beyond the world of employment. To look at society and see how it can be improved through new innovation.

NO 2: Thinking Negatively

Your negative thinking. (You never see anything good in anything).

Nothing kills good ideas faster than this. In fact, ideas are killed in their tracks long before they are even attempted or experimented on. A negative thinker believes that there is no use even trying, because it won't work. Having intoxicated your mind with negative notions, new exciting ideas pass under your nose without being noticed. You see other forging ahead and try to Ph.D. – pull him down – instead. To you, the glass will always be half empty, never half-full.

Instead of trying to find out why you can't get ahead in life, you opt to getting angry with the whole world. You firmly believe that the world owes you a living and when it fails to deliver what you want, you are inconsolable. You take your frustration out on others. Often the immediate family is the first victims. You even try to infect others with this bad habit so that you don't suffer alone.

NO. 3: Lack of Initiative

Your lack of imagination… (You will not even try to do anything without being told). Very few habits can beat lack of initiative.

As a proprietor of this habit, you firmly believe that nothing can be done unless you are told how to do it. Imagine the world with this kind of mind at the helm. The phone could never have been invented – forget the cell phone. Societies could permanently live in the past.

This kind of mind constantly says: I hope someone does something about this, that and the other. Instead of saying: I need to do something about it myself.

This kind of mind falters in the wind, instead of effecting the direction of the wind. This mind hoards knowledge and is responsible for all the bad things that have happened in this world. This mind condones evil by opting to look the other way.

NO 4: Lack of Ambition

Your lack of motivation. (You're satisfied with nothing).

Lack of ambition, means you sit back and become satisfied with nothing. You look around and begin judging your standard of living by those of your neighbors. Because your neighbors are not achievers, you find no reason to improve. You settle into your little world and actually convince yourself that it is all there is to life.

When you are called upon to change your life style for the better, you can see no good reason why you should. No amount of pressure can convince you otherwise.

Ever self-satisfied, you look back on life and wonder why you didn't do certain things when you were younger and stronger. Facing old age in abject poverty and misery, you frantically look for excuses to justify your lack of ambition.

They didn't rest on their laurels...

NO 5: Lack of Adventuring Spirit

You dwell in a world that is static. (Never experiment either on new ideas.) Ever heard the saying… nothing ventured, nothing gained?

Nothing good in this world has ever been achieved without the spirit of adventure. Neither in sciences or arts! Everything around us was achieved because someone took it upon himself or herself to venture the lonely route of discovery. The spirit of adventure enables us to look at our present circumstances and declare them inadequate, then actually seek to improve upon them. The adventurous mind propelled Thomas Alva Edison to discover the bulb; otherwise we would be still plunged in darkness.

People who lack adventuring spirit stop growing, show me someone who is not effective I will show you someone who has not learned anything new. You are what you are, you are where you are because of what is gone into your heart and mind. You only change in proportion to the people you meet and the places you go. Which is why you can get into small community and get narrow minded? You can drive back 20 years and nothing has changed and lot of people, business and corporate organization are just like that, what is lacking is the spirit of adventure.

The spirit of adventure drove Obafemi Awolowo, Jomo Kenyatta, Nelson Mandela and the others, to selflessly seek the freedom of their compatriots. The spirit of adventure, led Mother Theresa to the streets of Calcutta, India, so that the down-trodden of that country would have a chance in this world.

No. 6: Risky Not to Take Risks

You're a born again coward... (Will not try new ideas for fear of failure)

Your coming into this world was risky. Being conceived in your mother's womb and delivered safely was the greatest risk of all. Anything could have happened. So from today, take note that not to take risks in life, is itself a great risk.

Sitting on the sidelines ensure that all the good things in life belong to others – risk takers. You can only partake of them as a parasite. I want us to understand each other properly here. To take a risk in life should not mean that you ignore all the protocols of produce. It means you venture into something having first taken on board an arsenal of precautions.

Not taking any risks, means playing it safe. You deny yourself the opportunity to make a difference in this world. You inspire no new thinking nor do you influence society. You leave no legacy for future generations to look back on with admiration.

With all his failings as a human being, Mandela will bequeath this world a rich legacy of selflessness and dedication to the service of fellow humanity.

NO. 7: Petite Thinker

You live in a cave…. (You think small, plan small and achieve small).

No habit hinders progress more than thinking small. It ensures stagnation in life. You will always achieve little because you plan small. You will never get ahead because you plan small.

You will never appreciate new exciting ideas because they are above your head. You can't order to go for it. You can never change your circumstances for the better unless you migrate from your small world into a large one because all the actions are in that larger world.

The larger world is where good ideas exist, where opportunities are plentiful, where all great achievers live, where not even the sky is the limit.

No. 8: Procrastinator A Thief of Time

You're a negative researcher…. (There is always tomorrow).

Tomorrow simply never comes. Everything is tomorrow and tomorrow. You actually believe that the whole world is waiting for you.

You wait for tomorrow to do what you should have done last week. You lose so much time that you can never recover. Bear in mind that sometimes good opportunities knock at your door only once. They may never come back.

So when they do, seize the moment and jump into action. It is better to have tried and failed than never to have tried at all.

Nothing ventured, nothing gained.

NO. 9: The Blind Champion

You know not what they don't know… (Will not even seek to know)

What a terrible habit. It guarantees perpetual ignorance. It shuts you out of the world of adventure and discovery. Makes you a lonely island and prisoner of self-gratification and delusion.

A blind champion of doom who looks but won't see. Who feels but never thinks… who falters but never knows why… who labors ignorance but mistakes it for ingenuity….who possesses no panacea for the ups and downs of life save for what life itself has thrown at you…

NO. 10: Wrong Association

You swim with crocodiles but can't bite… (all your close friends lead mediocre lives).

Heard of the expression: 'Birds of the same feather flock together?' You are who you hang out with. If your company is made up of yobbos, then I'm afraid you won't fare much better either.

This group is always looking out for new recruits who are quickly initiated in the art of doing nothing to improve their lot. All the members must dress the same, think the same, live the same, perform the same, fail the same and be condemned by fate the same.

But contrast this situation with the company of self-motivated achievers. The dreamers are risk takers who shaped the world we live in, the thinkers who impacted positively on our lives, the brave and adventurous who were not afraid to try new ideas. They are the explorers who discovered new medical treatment so we can live longer and better lives and the inventors who made our lives easier (think of the cell phone and sliced bread).

No. 11: Fear of Failure

You seek approval…. (You live through others).

Fear of failure in itself is a state of mind which renders you a prisoner of inertia lacking in ambition. Fear relegates you to the status of a non-achiever for whom good things just pass by. This mentally denies you the opportunity to experiment with new ideas that can improve your standard of living. It designates you a captive, unable to think for yourself and must always seek approval from your master – fear. Fear of failure puts you in a permanent state of self-doubt and inadequacy.

It destroys your most potent asset; self-confidence. Without self-confidence you will always perform below par. You will always be the object of ridicule among your peers. You will never be entrusted with any mission. Your mind will always be crowned with negative thoughts which can only lead to more failure.

NO: 12: Inability to Separate Facts from Opinions

You listen only to what you want to hear… (Listening to chiefs none of whom are Indians) The wrong kind of advice is worse than no advice at all. Always assess the credentials of the person dishing out advice. Do these credentials check out?

A marriage guidance counselor, who has never been married, can hardly be the right person to advise about marriage, however knowledgeable he or she may be about the subject. A financial consultant who can hardly lay claim to seek self-made fortune, is not the right person to seek advice from about financial matters, even if he has a Ph.D. in Economics.

Learn to separate facts from opinions. Most people have mere opinions about things, but are very thin on actual facts. When a pilot talks to you about flying, you know you are listening to authority. When a lawyer talks to you about heart-transplant, however high esteem you know you are listening to opinions about this complex form of surgery.

No. 13: Expecting Somebody Else To Do It

You are lazy.…. (Get off your ass and do something).

Such people do exist in this world, they won't lift a finger and you are one of them. You expect everyone else to do for you. You want to harvest where you have not sown. You look for short cuts to wealth. You want to partake of all the goods in life without working for them.

Sorry, the real world doesn't quite work like that.

NO. 14: Too Arrogant for Progress

You are conceited… (You think you know it all).

This is your biggest undoing. Because you are conceited, you will not listen to new exciting ideas. Because of your arrogance, you assume you know better than the experts. You look down upon others. You assume (wrongly) that you know everything.

Listen, the reason you are so proud is because you have not really achieved anything in life. You hide this image to disguise your real self. Great achievers, such as Nelson Mandela, are the epitome of humility.

No habit estranges one from reality more.

No. 15: Without Listen Ears

You have no use for your own ears…... (You rather talk than listen).

Africans believe that the reason we have two ears and one mouth, is that we may listen twice as we talk. Listening is an art that can be learned. Learn to listen. Especially to new ideas. You never know better than you. It is a sure way of increasing knowledge.

I have a friend who when talking on the phone will have you believe that he has nodded off. When it is your turn to speak, his end of the line is dead silent. He never butts in with: yes-ha- ha; I see; quite right!' No, he listens intently.

Often he remembers what others said better than the authors themselves.

NO. 16: Deficient in Will, Determination & Courage

You lack guts… (You're a paper tiger).

You might have the most brilliant business ideas, without these three qualities, you will not get far.

The will is your strong desire to do it.

Determination means that 'no matter what happens you will carry through with your idea'. Courage gives you the strength to face a tiger bare handed if that is what it takes to achieve your dream.

Someone who aspires to be a world-boxing champion must have the fervent will to become world champion, the determination to go through with the rigors of training and the courage to face his opponent – unafraid.

Boxing legend Muhammad Ali possessed all these three qualities.

No. 17: Capitalizing On Your Handicapped

You are blind to your own resources… (Thinking you're as poor as a church mouse).

Please, stop it. Today! I don't care if you were born eyeless, legless, without arms or stone deaf or born into the poorest home on earth.

You are not poor at all.

What you probably mean is that you are not presently financially rich. But you are very wealthy in human potential. You are surrounded with tremendous resources. But poor in thought of exploiting those resources around you.

Some of the world greatest achievers were born so-called handicapped. But look what they achieved.

German Composer Ludwig Beethoven was born stone deaf. His compositions are classics.

American pop singer Steve Wonder was born blind. But that didn't stop him writing and singing beautiful songs.

Greek shipping magnet Aristotle Onassis was hopeless in mathematics at school. He went on to become a billionaire several times and over time learned how to count his billions.

Resources

Let us look at the huge resources surrounding you; the greatest being yourself and all the attributes the Almighty bequeathed you; i.e. your brain, your imagination and ability to perceive. These are tremendous resources which if properly exploited, can greatly alter your financial circumstance.

Your immediate family is a mighty resource to exploit positively. Your neighbours are an asset if you get on with them. Your colleagues at work are a resource. The stranger you encountered on the bus/train/plane could be turned into a resource. Your local club/church and any other association where people gather are potential resources. Your friends' friends and all their friends are a gold mine awaiting your exploitation. So where on earth is your poverty except in the way you think?

At a rough estimate, every human being knows on average well over one hundred thousand people. What a tremendous resource you didn't know you had.

Yes, I know you are wondering how? Here is how you know 100,000 people. You, yourself on average know about 500 people. These people in turn know another 500 people each as well. Then your immediate family, each knows a certain number of people. Your friends, your colleagues at work, name them. They know a certain number of people. All these people in turn know other people. If you assemble all those people, they would average 100,000.

No. 18: Habitual Liar

You're too dishonest and unreliable for your own good…. (Thinking you are smarter than everybody else)

This is a great let down.

Because you are so dishonest and unreliable, you won't get very far with your clients. People who deal with you must be assured that you are as good as your words – especially your last word.

There is always a chain reaction. If you let down a client, then that client will in turn, let down someone else. So your actions and omissions as a dishonest person may have far reaching consequences. Tell nine truths and one lie and you will always be remembered for that one lie.

No. 19: Scurry To Get Rich

You plant in the morning and expect to harvest in the evening….(want to run before you can walk).

Listen, not even the good Lord could deliver the world in one day. So take it easy. Walk the walk. Master the tricks of the trade as it were. Know almost all there is to know about your chosen idea. Research it, read about it. Study the market and the competition. Understand money and how to use it well. Never allow money to be your master.

All this will take time but at the end of it, you will be the master of your circumstances. It took a very long time to build Rome.

Back to money; the mistake most people make is to believe that if they had all the money in the world, they would have no other problem at all. Wrong! Wrong as it can be, some of the most miserable people in this world actually are very rich.

There are many people richer than the late billionaire; Chief MKO Abiola of Nigeria had all the money you may ever dream of in the world. Yes, they may be considered as richest men in the world. Yet some of these fellows are the most miserable fellows. Just imagine.

NO. 20: Bad News Carrier

You peddle bad news… (Nothing is ever good for you.)

You rejoice in other people's misery. You only say bad things about others. Because you clog your mind with bad news, all the positive things around, just pass you by.

You see only the bad, never the positive. Even if the business opportunity were placed right under your nose, you wouldn't see it. You would pretend not to see it so as to continue complaining.

No. 21: Overpowered By the Content in A Bottle

You drink too much… (Must always be the last to leave the bar). Alcohol consumed in small quantities now and then, like we have in our tooth pastes, bathing soaps, creams, perfumes and other essentials is not bad at all. But when you literally swim in it daily, then that is a misuse of your most vital resource – your brain. Nothing weakens and destroys brain cells faster than alcohol abuse. You waste money and time on alcohol - time that could be better spent building a successful future; money that could be better spent on a business.

NO. 22: Resentful of Successful People

You can't stand other people's success…. (Why them and not me)

You spend your best time and energies envying, instead of admiring and learning from successful people. For you, they are the reason you are so unsuccessful. You blame everyone for your lack of achievement – everyone else but yourself.

You can never achieve anything in life unless you first separate yourself from this negative and destructive emotion.

Why envy others when you don't know what they have gone through to become successful? You don't know the sacrifices, heartache and struggles they had to endure. Real success does not just fall from the sky- you have to work for it.

So learn from successful people.

No. 23: Lack of Focus

Every day, we are bombarded with hundreds of tasks, messages and people all competing for our time. This is why the ability to focus on your goal is so critical to achieving it. Focusing requires giving up some things in the present because you know the time invested will pay off big-time down the road. But the problem with many is that they have not given up those things that sharp their focus off.

Every day, ask yourself, "Is what I'm doing right now bringing me closer to my goal?" If it's not, do something that will. Focusing is like any habit: the more you do it, the easier it gets.

No. 24: Wrong Investment

You build on sand… (You trust on sight).

By all means judge a book by the cover, but read it as well. Many businesses go under because the owners put their trust in the wrong people. Only God can be trusted 100%.

Whoever you trust (on earth), must be judged by their actions and omissions, not by their looks.

Experience shows that the relative and business, like water and oil, don't always mix very well. You are forewarned.

No. 25: Constant Degrade Of Self

You put yourself down…. (I'm nothing).

You do it so often and so well that you have made a career out of it. What a great disservice to yourself. Your inferiority complex is a stumbling block to success. Never will you trust yourself to do anything great in life – nor would others. When you declare yourself as 'not good enough,' you give others ammunition with which to shoot you down.

From today you've got to start thinking and walking tall. Declare yourself the best thing

God ever put together and set out to accomplish your dreams.

Only you are best qualified to do this.

Abraham Lincoln never once looked down upon himself even though everyone else despised him. Instead, he continued believing in himself and his abilities – went on to become the president of the USA.

NO. 26: Living in an Expired World

You dwell in the past… (You are more fascinated by the past than the future).

I know you had a horrible childhood, but now is the time to migrate into a new orbit. Use your past to inspire you to climb to greater heights. It is not the depths whence you came that matters, but the heights you climb.

Only use the past to teach you about today, as you prepare for a much better tomorrow – much wiser.

No. 27: Concentration on Your Past History

You only count your problems… (Never your fortunes)

Just think of it; you are alive and well. You have a roof over your head. You are guaranteed three square meals a day. You probably have a loving family that cares for you dearly. The only time you come into contact with calamity is watching it on T.V, or reading about it in newspapers. Yet you have declared yourself the most unfortunate person on earth. You can't be serious.

By constantly showing ingratitude, you risk being denied the blessing that accompanies good fortunes. Confine the past to history and concentrate all your energies on the present for a better future.

No. 28: Only Talk! Talk and Talk Shop Show

You're a talker not a doer... (I can do this; I will do that; I plan to do it).

All you ever do is talk, talk and talk. But never do. You know so much about silence that you can talk about it for hours on end. Things happen because we make them to happen. Not because we talk them into happening. How can you call yourself a farmer and you never sow any seed.

A book is written by putting thoughts on paper. Talking is the advanced stage of thought. Doing however, is the final stage of the thought process. Mercifully, you have thought so that you may do good deeds.

No. 29: Blaming Others for Your State

You blame others for your failures… (It is not my fault I was born poor).

This is what lazy people do. They drown their sorrows in blaming the whole world but never themselves for their own failures. You also draw comfort from the fact that others will acknowledge that someone else is to blame, you always pass the buck. You live in a dream world – wake up!

The reason you are a failure is because you have chosen (yes, chosen) to be a failure. You have abdicated your responsibility. Have chosen to place your life in other people's hands and surrendered your personal empowerment.

No. 30: Too Proud To Ask For Help

You wallow in ignorance …. (I don't want to look a fool).

By not asking for help and advice you will end up looking foolish anyway.

The most stupid question is the one not asked. By not asking questions, you cannot learn from those who know better than you do. Many will rather blunder than ask for help.

Very few people realize the wisdom embedded in asking questions. Far from the habit exposing your ignorance, it reveals your intelligence. The habit further enables you to access knowledge quickly, saving you a lot of research time and money.

No. 31: Careless About Tomorrow

You live from day to day… (The future will take care of itself).

You do not think about the future, so you can hardly plan for it. You mistakenly believe the future will take care of itself. As the seconds tick away and months turn into years, the future closes in on you and before long, it is right before you. Completely unprepared, you must deal with it, often painfully.

By squandering your youth today, you risk paying dearly in old age tomorrow.

No. 32: Wasting Time on Uncreative Things

You invest in dead stock… (Let the good times roll).

You must watch every soap opera on TV; attend every function in town; be seen at every funeral procession; attend every disco. You are the chairperson of every association that springs up; you are on the committee of fifty other organizations. You must go shopping every Saturday afternoon because all your friends do that. You must watch every new movie Hollywood comes up with and like clockwork, hit the disco floor every single Friday night. Have you ever heard of setting priorities in life?

But you will need to do what the Bible says and 'let the dead bury the dead.'

No. 33: Receiving and Receiving Only

You have a welfare mentality… (Most people are kind and will help me).

So you are nothing but a leach that wallows in living off others. You have neither self- respect nor self-esteem. Neither do you have any modicum of decency to speak of.

You take but never give back. You harvest but never sow

You want to partake of the fruits of labor to which you contribute absolutely nothing. You

Harvest Where You Have Not Sown.

You have no right to demand or expect respect from others. You are the epitome of the worst habits in humanity. I have nothing but utter contempt for you. I am sorry, but this is how I feel about you.

NO. 34: Being A Waster of Time

Your world is disorganized … (you plan on being late for your own funeral). You are always late for appointments. Even the ones you set up.

You never deliver what you promise on time. You never turn up when expected.

You never answer letters, nor return calls.

You procrastinate about everything under the sun. You Squander People's Time not. You are personally responsible for all the good things that should have been done, but were Shame – shame, upon you!

No 35: Users and Opportunists

You only use people to get things and then you dump them, looking for how you can walk on others to get to your destination. Ruthless in doing this you can go to any length no matter who the person is.

Think about how many people you have used and dumped with this attitude it would be difficult for you to become an outstanding person even if you become one it would not last.

No 36: Very Unstable Mind

You would rather worry than think… (You are a born-again worrier)

The moment you hit a problem, you must worry yourself to death. Long before you have explored and exhausted all means of solving the problem, you sink into worry.

Worry sends the wrong signal to the brain and destabilizes it. In this state of anxiety, the brain fails to concentrate or reason rationally. All bad decisions are as a result of worry – not careful thought.

CHAPTER 4

THE BALANCE PLAN

Your Valuable Asset

Your biggest and most valuable asset is your potential.

Within you, lies tremendous potential that can propel you towards success. In very vein of your body, there is potential waiting to be unlocked; hitherto untapped resources that you could use to your advantage.

You believe so-called 'experts' who told you that you are not good enough; that you are not cut out for certain things. Absolute garbage! The truth is, you are uniquely gifted in your own unique way. Every human being was created with certain capabilities. True, some with more than others. But anyone with a functioning brain can apply himself or herself to any task and actually accomplish it. It is a mental game. The human mind if tuned properly can be trained to accomplish anything. All it takes is the fervent desire to achieve your dream in this world.

You must have a dream. Be dedicated to that dream Live that dream every single day of the week.

At eleven years old, Harold Wilson had a dream of becoming Prime Minister of Great Britain. He even had his picture taken in front of 10 Downing Streets (official residence of British Prime Minister.) Guess what? He would go on to become one, thirty-some years later. In part five there is a list of proven business ideas to choose from Business ideas that have made other people fabulously rich. Pick a business idea that best suits your circumstances. Research that idea thoroughly. Know all there is possibly to know about the idea. Learn from the real experts. Read whatever you can lay your hands on. Ask a lot of questions. Remember the potential within you is unlimited. When properly tapped and unleashed, it can help you succeed at whatever you put your hands to.

The Great Thing Locked Up Within You

Maybe you were meant to be the greatest business person that ever lived…if only you had tried your hand at business. Maybe you were cut out to be the greatest inventor… if only you had put your mind to some new innovation. May be you were meant to be the best actor Hollywood has ever seen… if only you had given theater a thought. May be you were meant to be the best writer that ever lived… if only you had put some thought to paper. May be you were born to be the greatest singer… if only you had cared to join the local choir. May be you were meant to be the greatest painter… if only you had persevered with a brush and canvas. May be you were to be the next Mandela… if only you had dedicated yourself to the cause of humankind.

Within us all, there is hidden talent somewhere that can only surface if we dare dream and put it into action.

Adjust Your Life

In order to pursue your dream wholeheartedly, some changes are going to be necessary.

You can't continue as the same person you were before - that old you were, a non-achiever, small thinker and failure in life. The new you are, a big thinker, dreamer and achiever driven.

Instrument for Success

Now that your mind is freed of those toxic chemicals, let us embark on a course of action. Let us start our exciting journey to make money. Believing that we can make it; that victory is ours for the taking.

Now is the time to take matters in your own hands. To take on the bull by the horns. There is one person and one person only, best qualified to do this. One person who (with the help of God) can make it happens. That person is your good self-reading this book right now.

But like everything else in life, we need to be properly armed. We need some tools to take with us on this fascinating journey.

Take Life Action Plan

This plan of action calls for some difficult adjustments in your life. You will have to retune your mind to third differently. You have to let go of some bad habits in the name of your dream and acquire new and better ones. You will have to stop smoking, drinking, gambling and whatever else that might stand in the way of your progress.

You may have to lose some old friends and acquire new ones. You need friends that think like you now. Who have also decided to greatly change their circumstances for the better? You might have to relocate. To move to an area, town, city or country that will offer you better opportunities to pursue your dream. You might have to go back to school (parallel degree programmes are offered in almost every university in Kenya presently) and take some evening classes to learn more about this new idea you have taken on.

You may have to sell off something very dear to you in order to move on. You may have to change your life style and become a completely new person to suit your new circumstances, by getting up earlier than usual, starting a regime of exercise and changing your diet as well. You might need to acquire a completely new wardrobe - a wardrobe that announces you as a successful person.

If you are married or have a partner, I suggest you bring them on board. So you have two powerful resources pushing in the same direction. Strengthen your fronts in the battle and attack as mighty force.

Who but yourself can stop you?

Do Away With Unhealthy Habits

This is absolutely essential. These bad habits were responsible for your lack of development. Continuing with them will only curtail your progress.

If you never spent one minute thinking and analyzing issues, now is the time to do so. If you have never visited your local library, spare time to register now. If you never frequented bookstores before, this is the time to find out which new ideas are on the market. If you have never consulted on finances or business in general, now is your best chance to do so. If you never gave the future a thought (because you lived one day at a time) it is the time to wake up. If you drink little or much, stop and give alcohol a break.

Go For Healthy Habits

With a bit of ingenuity, you can do it easily. As you think differently so you acquire new attitudes to life. And without thinking, act differently. You acquire certain new habits to become much more self-disciplined than previously. You might have to take on a whole new culture in order to feel comfortable with your new life.

Connect Yourself with Progressive Friends

As the saying goes: birds of a feather flock together, seek out the kind of friends who are like-minded; friends who are up and about building better futures for themselves and their families. Friends who think progress, dream success, work for successes, which are honest and straight. Those are the kind of people you need to hang around with.

Those who have resigned themselves to whatever Mother Nature throws at them are out. Get rid of them today and move on.

Change Your Location

This might need real guts. It is not always easy to start life in a new place. But if that is what it is going to take for you to achieve your goals, so be it as human beings we are inclined not to appreciate our own backyard.

New surroundings excite our minds and challenge us to see what the natives don't. Deprived of the small town we grew up in, or own country, we are much more likely to make a go of it. No more relatives or friends to turn to, we look within to tap our own resources.

So, if it is Lagos or Lusaka where your dream will be exploited, don't hesitate to venture there. Get information about the town. Get in touch with people you may know there. If you want to venture outside the country, say to Japan, go to the nearest Japanese consulate and find out about relocating to Japan. If you have friends living in Japan, they will be placed to give you the inside picture of that country.

However, I would strongly advise paying a fact-finding visit to Japan first before you make a final decision about setting there. Your will see things with your own eyes!

Change Your Appearance

You are what you wear. Dull and dreary clothes will announce you as boring and unsuccessful. Donate them to Salvation Army today.

Nobody wants to associate with a failure. I suggest you visit a fashion expert for some tips on how to look successful. Or simply browse the fashion magazines. Look out for successful people. See how they dress and carry themselves. And please pay particular attention to personal hygiene.

You might be the smartest person in town bubbling with new exciting ideas, but body odor might look against you.

Look great, smell wonderful and the whole world will want to know you.

Be an Early Riser

My experience is that the earlier the better. Personally, I religiously wake up at 5 0'clock in the morning. Do my morning readings. At 7 I look at the daily papers. All being well and equal, I proceed to make my prayers. I ask God's forgiveness for all the sins committed during the previous day and promise not to go through with the ones I intended to commit in the future.

At that time, most of the world is still asleep, so God is free and listens to me more attentively. He usually lets me off with a warning. I next proceed to bang away one or two pages on my PC and then go to the bathroom.

By waking up early, you add more time to your day. Achievers on the move accomplish more by getting up early in the mornings.

People with loosing attitudes say I can't, People with winning attitudes says I will try. The difference is the mindset. Millionaire says I will make time out, losers says I have no time. Winners say it is worth trying, a loser says it won't work. Millionaire says I owe life, losers says life owes me. Winners says I am glad to help, losers says it is not my job. Winners say I will do my best, losers say I don't do that. The world is full of losers who say I do not do this or that, but what do you do? Because there are people who get up early every day and go ahead to do those things that losers dodged and become successful in life. A loosing attitude will keep you from reaching your full potential that God has created you with.

Routine Exercise

Nothing beats less weight and agility. It makes life much easier; a healthy body, a healthy mind. So please, get yourself into a routine of exercise. You will feel better, sleep better and stay better focused longer.

Start with light exercises about the house like stretches and skipping. Then slowly graduate to jogging in the mornings, or go to the gym. You will soon see a difference.

"Now you know why your neighbor has such a great shape".

Go for the Biggest

Why not? That is what big thinkers do.

Big thinkers take on bigger tasks. They take risks. They go the longer route. They assign themselves more responsibilities. They climb taller mountain – not tiny hills. They feel challenged by obstacles placed in their way and go on to overcome them.

At the end of it all, they are well grounded polished and eager to take on even bigger tasks.

All the best things happened because someone bit off more than they could chew. They set greater challenges to prove their abilities.

IN A NUTSHELL

*Take bigger Challenges
*Have a Ready Made Plan.
*A game plan is the modus operandi.

You need to structure your business plan in such a way that is easy to understand and as follows:

Whoever is associated with you must be able to understand it as well. This is the road map to your financial success. It has to be carefully thought out. Lay out a strategy that will see to the highs and lows of your business. Find out where competition falls.

Many businesses encounter difficulties, because no clear plan was put in place to deal with problems that are sure to come up.

Prevention is always better than cure.

*Lay out A Strategy for the Lows.
*Research before You Make a Move.

Don a detective's hat and get to work. Go out investigate the line of business you are interested in you might encounter a business idea you had not previously thought about, an idea that works for you. So have an open mind.

Introduce yourself as a researcher, finding out about a particular business. The owners will enthusiastically talk about themselves and???

The Qualification Required

The narrower meaning is paper qualification alone. You need more than just paper qualification to succeed in business, you need:

*Honesty;
*Hard work, innovation;
*Agility of the mind;
*Dedication;

*Commitment;
*To be affable,
*To be approachable;
*To be easy to work with,
*To be well organized,
*To be tactful with people;
*To be thick skinned;
*Good public relations;
*Patience;
*Tolerance'
*Politeness;
*Ambition and self-drive;
*To be resourceful; to be smart (intelligent)
*To be far sighted;
*To be skillful;
*To be persuasive;
*Ingenuity.

These are just some of the credentials you need to be armed with, to have chances in business.

IN A NUTSHELL

Be a Leader

Impeccable credentials will do more for you than any amount of Money you can invest in it. Be a Leader. Business people are leaders in their own right. They impact our lives every single day of the week. They determine what we eat, the cloths we wear, car we drive and the home appliances we can't do without. Even the type of medication prescribed to us by our family doctor, is partially influenced by business people. Because of their great influence in our lives, they must be highly responsible. They have to be men and women of integrity whose reputations are beyond reproach.

So as you go into business bearing in mind that you are not just to be another businessman or woman, but a leader as well. A leader whose actions and omissions affected society.

Greek shipping magnet, Aristotle Oniassis, was a leader. His charges for freight goods around the world impacts on prices at your supermarket.

Aim To Be an all Exemplary Business Leader

Travel with Principle

It should come with the territory. Being principled means that there are certain things you will do and things you will not do-on principle. When a customer is not satisfied, repair the damage at your expense. When your crooked accountant suggests you fix the books to beat the system; you say, 'no' and fire him/her on the spot. When a tax evader tries to sell you unaccustomed goods, you send them packing. That is what principled people do.

*When a customer returns goods, either replace them or refund the money unconditionally.

Get Yourself Together

You can always see a disorganized business with your eyes closed: Books are not well kept; Bills are not paid early; Orders are not delivered as promised'; Employees are not paid on time; Receipts are not issued for goods sold, Correspondence is never answered on time, or at all, The inventory (stock) is not well documented, Customers are turned away for goods not available, etc

Have profile of your business written and printed out to be handed to customers especially new ones. A profile should clearly state what you do, how you do it and the general company policy. Let the information include the names and addresses of companies you have done business with. This is important for reference purposes. New and prospective customers can easily check up on your credibility. One good work from a satisfied customer will do wonders for the image of your business. Please include your future plans as well. This will show that you are a big thinker going places.

Have a website expert design a professional site for your business. This is the age of the

Internet and you don't want to be left behind. Answer All Correspondents.

Boost the Ego of Others

We all have egos- some bigger than others. We all need to be praised and have our egos stroked from time to time. Being in business means interacting with people of all kinds, some with real massive ego problems.

Whenever you have to interact or negotiate with anyone put your interest and your ego on hold for a while. Centre the conversation on the other person – not yourself. Talk about his/her business interests and achievements. Pay tribute to their ingenuity and business acumen. Congratulate them on their entrepreneurial skills. People enjoy talking about themselves and their achievements. Ask for advice. Advance your cause slowly and subtly. A stroked ego is fertile ground on which to nurture a mutually beneficial business relationship.

That nothing – looking secretary to the boss, security guard to a building or receptionist in an office, will gradually do whatever you want when you have stroked their ego first by simply being nice to them.

Master the Know-how of Whatsoever Your Hand Finds

The word 'tricks' should not be negatively interpreted to mean cheating your clients – a futile exercise in business. If you do, sooner than later, you will be caught out. Learning the 'tricks of the trade' means mastering the ins and outs of your chosen business. That you know all there is to know. Like sourcing your products in such a way that you have great leverage as far as profits are concerned.

When times are hard (as they often are), you structure your prices downwards and still make a profit. When competition raises prices; you give a discount and be able to survive at the same time. When there is scarcity of a certain product you are well supplied with it.

When competition charges for delivery; you offer free delivery service. When competition has a 'GOODS ONCE SOLD NOT RETURNED' sign posted outside their shop; you put a notice that reads, MONEY BACK GURANTEE ON ALL GOODS RETURNED. – no questions asked!

Good business management is about being smart. Don't follow the crowd. These are just some of the tricks of the trade. Be a Salesman. Whether you like it or not, you are now a salesman. The fact that you didn't go to Harvard Business School, should not be a handicap. You too can learn the techniques that make a great salesman;

Don't limit your horizons. Never assume anything about anybody. Never underestimate the consumer's knowledge of what they buy with their hard-earned money.

Know your products inside out. Don't leave home without good manners in your briefcase as well. And remember to apply them.

Always be sensitive to the needs of the customer – your boss! Always ask all to buy. Knock on all doors. Never, and never argue with a customer. Always aim to satisfy the customer by offering back guarantee. Always call back on your customer – especially after a sale.

Understand Your Market

At the end of the day, it all boils down to marketing. Study the market fastidiously. Aim to improve upon it rather than duplicate what is already there.

If you don't understand your market, who does? Knowing and understanding the market will dictate what to sell and how to sell it better. Improve on quality, performance and service where possible. Advertise and advertise whatever you sell better. Improve on quality, performance and service where possible. People are more likely to buy what they have seen or heard of.

Remember, Coca-Cola is the most famous and easily recognizable beverage on earth. Why? Because it is vigorously marketed through promotion and advertisement. Leave no stone unturned in this crucial area of business.

Advertise Your Business. People Buy What They Know. Keep A Charming Personality

Always be a charmer – it costs nothing. Your friendly, charming personality will always win you friends and influence people. It is an asset that augurs well for business. It is the ultimate ticket to your clients' hearts, the key to your bank manager's vault. It will help to keep the creditors at bay until you're able to pay up.

This is what separates you from the crowds. And finally, what will keep customers flooding your way. By all means read, How to Make Friends and Influence People by Dale Carnegie. Being Charming costs nothing but pays handsome dividends.

CHAPTER 5

GREAT IDEAS THAT EARN YOU MONEY TODAY

Headed for Improved Ideals

This world needs people with ideals. Too many drift through life having no standard and no ideals to beckon them forward. Ideals are an essential for progress. They goad us out o f lethargy and self-complacency. If some people had not been idealist s we should still be clothing ourselves with skins. The inventor and the reformer keep the clock of progress ticking.

You may not claim to be in either of these categories, but you will find it helpful to have your own ideals.

Firstly, hold the ideal of perfect health for yourself. Do not be content to limp through life dogged by constant ailments. Do not be like the people who expect poor health and who get it! Be sure to read the first chapter of this book again.

Next, be an idealist regarding your own personality. Aim at completeness, harmonious development – in a word, maturity. Jesus of Nazareth encouraged people to be idealists. 'Be ye perfect,' He is recorded to have said, 'even as your Father in heaven is perfect.'

Too many people are content to remain undeveloped and childish in their emotions, reactions and characteristics. Some will pride themselves upon their fiery temper, forgetting that when they were young such outbursts were called tantrums. Others will become bullies in the office whenever something isn't going their way, failing to recognize they are acting like a spoilt child. Many adults retain the arrogance of youth, with its intolerance, impatience and lack of understanding. Some remain entirely egocentric like some children; they never look beyond the confines of their own hope and desires.

To keep before you the ideal of a full-orbed character will act as an incentive and impel you forward towards maturity. Don't rest content while you can find with yourself any traces of the juvenile. Cultivate patience, tolerance, and understanding. Develop always the wide view, broad sympathies and generous interpretation.

Self-knowledge will help you towards this ideal. To be able to recognize the different ingredients of your own human make-up will increase your self-mastery and keep you from the snap judgment or uncharitable condemnation.

Thirdly, be an idealist regarding your mind. Be ambitious to keep it keen, sensitive and aware. There is much around you to encourage coarseness and lethargy, so cultivate an ear for what is good and beautiful. Seek only the best in the arts. Observe the wonders and beauties of nature – the ever-changing pageant of the skies, the fragrance of flowers, the grace of trees, the innocence of children, the laughing eyes of a girl in love. Look, too, for beauty in the characters of others – unselfishness, courage, patience, cheerfulness, sympathy.

If you don't already love it, turn again to poetry. Forget your youthful prejudices and make a genuine attempt to enjoy it. Remember, it should be read aloud; and you will appreciate a poem only when you understand its every reference. A poet is especially sensitive to beauty and more aware than most of what is going on around him. If you tarry with him, he cannot but improve the quality of your mind.

Not only poetry but also the prose works of the elite of the ages will refine the mind. Knowledge of history too, will make its own contribution.

Your commonsense will tell you that there are some areas of life where the pursuit of an ideal might cause distress and unhappiness.

Watch out for these "Nevers"

The first is in marriage. Never expect your partner to measure up to your ideal. Paragons do not exist. You must expect to find failings in your partner. It is just possible you have a few yourselves!

Secondly, never expect your employment to be ideal in every respect. There are snags in the best of jobs. Those who would not change their work if they could, admit this.

Thirdly, don't expect to find a place to live where everything comes up to your dreams. Instead, concentrate on those aspects which satisfy you and forget the others.

With these exceptions, there is a place for idealism in life so long as you do not become a perfectionist. Such people are unrealistic and unhappy. Most important: Confine your ideals to your own behavior and activities and do not demand them of others.

77 Fortunes Making Ventures

1-Manufacturing

When you are a manufacturer of a product or products, you are the ultimate boss. You are the origin. You determine the price. In spite of the challenges that come with the territory, no approach to business offers you a better opportunity to make money. Look around for an item in great demand research how to manufacture it and improve on it.

If it is a knockout idea, there is always OPM-Other People's Money. Banks are only too eager to finance projects they believe are a safe bet.

READ Made in Japan (Fontana/Collins, 1987) the story of SONY by Akio Morita with
Edwin M. Reingold and Mitsuko Shimomura.

2-Energy

Whatever area of energy you get into, you are bound to make it. Why? Because the whole world operates on energy. Factories need energy. Planes in the sky, ships on the seas, trains and vehicles – all run on energy, our homes – whether rich or poor-use some form of energy. There is simply no end.

READ: Getty – The Richest man in the world (Grafton Books 1985) by Robert Lenzer.

3- Fashion

The whole world wears clothes. Whether out freezing cold, on the sports field or on the beach. All humanity needs to look their best.

4-Food

We need to eat – every single day of the week. Research your idea and find the right location. Fast foods seem to be very popular everywhere in the world. Diet foods are gainingcurrency in Africa today, especially in the big cities in the continent. Do not forget traditional foods as well.

5- Jewelry

Gold, diamonds and other precious stones will always be in great demand. All those weddings and engagements that take place every day around the world need these precious metals and gems to spice up the occasion. There is money to be made in custom Jewellery as well.

6- Real Estate

This is a solid business. Banks would quickly finance real estate than any other business around. You can disappear from the face of the earth, but buildings will not easily disappear.

7- Export & Import

This can be lucrative business if handled properly. Find out what the country where you live does not produce or manufacture and research the area of business. Likewise find out what it produces or manufactures in excess and find market for those products. Export them to the counties that needed them. Some fellows are ranking in money in what they call "fishing flies" – for export.

8- Computers

Almost everything within the world of Computers is paying. Whether computer software's, programming, providing Internet services, website, designing, computer spare parts or sales and accessories can be paying. Ask Bill Gates.

READ: Anything on Bill Gates of Microsoft Computers.

9- Shipping

The entire world survives on shipping. Goods must be freighted around the world twenty four hours a day, three hundred and sixty five days a year. Whether you actually own ship(s) or not, become a shipper's agent clearing and forwarding, you can't go too wrong. One Aristotle Onassis was the only a billionaire out of shipping.

READ: Aristotle Onassis (Weidenfeld and Nicolson) by Mark Otterway and Lewis Chester.

10- Perfume and Cosmetics

Who in his or her right mind does not want to smell gorgeous? Most people (especially women) must use perfumes and cosmetics every single day. Este'e Lauder of the Este'e Lauder Perfume fame, was once asked how much money had she amassed over the years manufacturing perfume and cosmetics? She replied simply, 'Too much'.

READ: Anything on Este'e Lauder of Este'e Lauder cosmetics and Skin Care Products fame.

11- Medicine (Pharmaceuticals) and Herbal

We all need this service at one point or another. Either manufacturing or sales, this is by far one of the fastest growing businesses in the world. Every week, a disease crops up. Medicine must be found to treat it. Need I say more? Perhaps add that medically proved herbal medicine to maintain HIV/Aids are in great demand in Zambia.

READ: The Life of James Goldsmith (Grafton, 1987) Geoffrey

12-Spare Parts

Our appliances and other gadgets must break down from time to time. Motor spare parts especially, will always be in great demand.

13-Electronics

We need to be entertained. All sorts of gadgets are needed to achieve this end. Can you imagine life without the electric kettle, the cooker or the fridge? How about the iron and all sorts of gadgets we seem unable to live without.

READ: Made In Japan (Fontana/Collins, 1987) the story of SONY by Akio Morita with

Edwin M. Reingold and Mitsuko Shimomura.

14-Hospitality Industry

Hotels, lodges, resorts and restaurants are part of our everyday life. Public relations is the key. Well planned and targeted, there is money to be made in this industry.

READ: Anything on Conrad Hilton of the Hilton chain of hotels.

15-Torism

That annual holiday humanity can't do without, translates into tourism. Offer reasonably priced package tours and you are in big business. Here, customer satisfaction is the key. This can be all year round business providing you keep up with the different seasons around the world.

16-Wholesale

If you are to get into wholesale business, it is often better than retail. If you have what retailers want at competitive prices then you will sell goods in greater volumes. Accountability is also a lot easier.

17-Used Cars

Selling quality used cars is a great business. Not all humanity can afford new cars. Give your customers a good deal and they will tell all their friends about you.

18-Haulage Services

Goods must be transported to and from ports to customers. Make a name by being reliable and you will always be in demand.

19-Funeral Services

This is often ignored by most people (because of its macabre nature) but highly lucrative. People die- funeral services are needed every day. So whether you offer mortuary services, you will be in demand three-hundred –sixty-days-six days a year!

20-Transport

People must travel every day. Whether by air, sea, road, rail, humanity is on the move. Offer clean, reliable services and you will laugh all the way to the bank.

21-Supplying Agricultural Implements

Food and other crops must be grown. Fertilizers, farms machinery and their spare parts will always be in demand. So what on earth are you waiting for?

22-Communication

Anything to do with communication is a hot cake. Take the cell phone for example. This form of communication has revolutionized the communication industry. Look around yourself and what is every human being armed with? So whether it is the equipment itself, accessories, airtime or offering Internet services, you can't go wrong in communication business.

23-Insurance

Insurance of vehicle and buildings is a legal requirement. In some cases you require life insurance before you can be employed by a company or secure a loan. All this translates into big business.

READ: All You Can Do Is All You Can Do (Oliver Nelson, 1988) Br A.L. Williams.

24-Office Supplies

Whether machinery in general, stationery or other paraphernalia required in offices, is a very lucrative area.

25-Stationery

The world lives on stationery, books, newspapers, magazines and you name it, are needed every day of the week. Where could you possibly go wrong in this business?

26-Printing & Publishing

Whether magazines, books, newspapers, office stationery, business cards, T-shirts – all need to be printed. Seek to have long-term contracts. Printing of school books and selling ream papers is particularly lucrative.

READ: Anything on Rupert Murdock and John H. Johnson of Ebony Magazine fame.

27-Catering Services

Always in demand; weddings, birthdays, anniversaries, conferences, graduations and funerals all require catering services.

28-Counselling Services

The world is full of all sorts of problems. Both in personal life and in general. If you can claim expertise in a certain specialized area that requires counseling services, then you are in a money-mining business. Also writing a book on that subject will set you apart from the others.

29-Nursing Services

Hospitals cannot always cope with every demand. The aged and invalid need specialized attention. The very rich demand personalized attention when sick. Specialized but excellent area of business.

READ: Anything on Florence Nightingale founder of the nursing profession.

30-Selling

Great business. There is simply no end to selling. You can just about sell anything to anybody anytime. This is actually my favorite pass time apart from writing. All you need is excellent public relations and tact with people.

READ: How to master the Art of Selling (Grafton Books) by Tom Hopkins.

32-Writing

Well what can I say about writing? I live by it. If you took writing away from me I would die. It is the oxygen that keeps me going. You may choose to write books; or articles for newspapers and magazines. There is also a lucrative area in ghost writing. Some people have stories to tell, but can't write them, so hire experts to do it for them. You could become that expert.

READ: How to write a million dollars book proposal (Organ books) by Chief M. Nangoli. READ: On writing well (Harper Perennial, 1998) by William Zinsser.

33-Financial Services

Anything to do with money can't be bad. Whether you advise people about finance or arrange personal loans, mortgages and you name it – you can't go wrong. Here, word of caution. You better have monies of your own to ward off the temptation of dipping your hands in the till, as it were. Other peoples' money is always sweeter.

34-Antiques & Art Collection

The value of antiques always goes up-never down. As for art itself, you never know what that innocuous painting hanging on your wall might be worth. Especially when the painter dies and achieves fame posthumously.

Dutch painter Vincent Van Gough was so poor that he literary ate from garbage bins. He achieved notoriety after his death and today the cheapest of his masterpieces will set you back a whopping thirty – million shillings.

35-Mail Order

People nowadays are too busy to go out shopping. So identify items that can be sold through mail order and specialize in that. Set up a special account for this venture and never touch a cent until the customer has received and is satisfied with goods.

36-Selling on the Internet

This automatically gives you access to the global market. It is a booming market. The products get exposed to the entire population of Internet surfers.

READ: Anything on Amazon.com

37-Cleaning Services

Set upon office cleaning services and offer reasonable rates and efficient services. You will never be out of work.

38-Gardening Services

Most people dream of having that heavenly garden to relax in. With a bit of creativity and innovation, you can design unique gardens that will advertise your services. A beautiful garden will advertise itself and your services as well to passersby-free of charge.

39-Pet Foods

If you work out the world population of domestic pets and multiply it by two five hundred grams of tins of food per pet, per day – it adds up to millions of tons of tinned pet food. How could you possibly go wrong on that kind of business?

40-Soft Drinks

There are more teetotalers in this world than drunkards. Need I say more?

41-Farming

If you have a calling to farming, then go for it. It is a long time business. Research your area and get orders for your produce before you start. Food business will never go out of business.

42-Vineyards

Apart from soft drinks, wine the second most consumed beverage in the world. Supplying grapes to wine makers is an ever expanding business.

43-Multi-Level Marketing

This revolutionary way of marketing products gives you the opportunity to build a residual income. Residual incomes means you supply goods on repeat basis and earn a percentage income from them for life. An author earns from his/her work as long as it sells.

READ: The Possible Dream – the story of Amway by Paul Con.

READ: How to become an organic millionaire through Amway & GNLD (Organic Books) by Chief M. Nangoli.

44-Dating Services

The need for this service can't be overemphasized. Today, there are more singles in need of this service than ever before. This is a singles rescue service.

45-General Agencies

This service is highly marketable. People feel more comfortable transacting business through professionals. It is assumed that an 'agent' knows best and will get a better deal for his/ her client.

46-Editing & Indexing Services

Free-lance editing and indexing is in a great demand. Building writers and even seasoned ones are always looking out for professional help.

47-General Construction

You need to work with your client closely and over a long period of time. Much as you are the 'expert', listen aggressively to the special wants and needs of your clients. Customer satisfaction is a must. This is another great business that really pays, especially when you establish a name for yourself.

48-Packing

This is an important service to manufactures who want their product to look good. Offer quality services and you will always be in demand. There is simply no limit to this business.

49-Massage Services

Most professionals are stressed. They need to relax with a massage. Better if you are also able to take these services to the workplace. That is where you will encounter most stressed humanity.

50-Shopping and Delivery Services

There are an awful number of people who for one reason or another, can't go shopping. Offer this service and you will be addressing a special need.

51-Fruits & Vegetables

The number of vegetables around the world will soon overtake carnivorous humanity. An increasing number of people are also becoming health conscious. They are responding to their doctors' clarion: eat more fruits and vegetables.

52-Maintenaace (Domestic)

Appliances are always breaking down around the home. Whether it is blocked pipes or a leaking roof. Offer twenty-four hours emergence service. Advertise yourself in offices around town. Be easily reachable, efficient and affordable. Big money!

53-Security Services

It's a highly specialized type of business with increasing demand. As people become wealthier and acquire more possessions, so they need others to protect them. Personal protection for a certain breed of people is also profitable.

54-Door –To- Door Selling

Great way to earn a living if you can do it. I did it for a while. All you need is a thick skin, tact with people and remarkable public relations. (PR) skills – that is the easy part. You also need patience, a sense of humor and tons of guts-as you will be knocking on strangers' doors. I have lost count of how many times I had the door slammed in my face. Keep your beard trimmed lest you mistaken for one of Bin Laden's disciples.

However, this business only becomes lucrative when you create repeat customers' by building a large clientele to supply with either the same things or new products – on regular basis.

55-Fashion Designing

There is simply no end to the world of fashion. Especially where women are concerned. Decide on the market you want to target. Come up with unique and innovative styles and you can make a bundle.

56-Food & Production Processing

How could you go wrong? Being perishables you must be careful about processing and preservation. Don't cut corners. Adhere to strict standards of hygiene.
READ: Anything on Gail Borden of Borden Mild and Ice Cream fame.

57-Herbal Medicine

A growing market as Chinese herbal medicine has demonstrated. People are turning to herbal medicine in large numbers due to less toxicity and side effects.

58-Keep Fit Services

More people around the world are becoming health conscious. Apart from starting a gym, explore the possibility of setting up keep – fit classes in work places. Most office workers can't find the time to go to the gyms – nail them in their place of work.

59-Lobbying

If you are well connected, lobbying at government level can be quite paying. Usually working on commission basis, where some deals run into millions of shillings.

60-Mineral Prospecting

Highly specialized field but enormously paying. It is usually large corporations or governments that require theses services. Your professional fee will be no problem for a country interested in mine prospecting.

61-Oil Prospecting

Almost along the same lines as mineral prospecting. The best in this highly risky but equally lucrative business is to negotiate a royalty fee every liter extracted.

READ: Getty – The Richest Man In The World (Grafton Books 1985) by Robert Lenzner.

READ: The Rockefeller, An American Dynasty (Jonathan Cape) by Peter Colllier and Davied Horrowtiz.

62. Investing on the Stock

Easily one of the smart ways of multiplying your money (risks not withstanding) Consult with a renowned stockbroker before you take the plunge

READ: Tycoon- The Life of James Goldsmith (Grafton, 1987) by Geoffrey Wansell.

63-Buying Shares in Companies

First investigate the soundness and viability of the company. How long has it been in business? Who do you know that has bought shares in that company? How did they fare? All being equal, you should yield great returns from buying shares. I highly recommend it.

64-Hair Salon Services

Another necessary need and some ladies' favorite pass-time. Men are fast catching up. Go for it.

65-Carpentry/Joinery

Most homes and offices could do with more innovative and creative furniture. Be unique in style and advertise. You will be in demand.

66-Day Care Services

As more and more young mothers feel the need to go out to work, so there is an increasing need for this service. The beauty of it is also that you can do it within the confines of your home. In some countries you have to register with the relevant authorities.

67-Frieghting Kids To and Fro from School

Most people hate getting up early to take kids to school. Take advantage of this need. Another business idea for which you do not need business premises. All you need is reliable means of transport.

68-Secretariat Services

Most people neither have the time nor the 'know-how' when it comes to secretarial work. Invest in a computer, photocopier and stationery and you are in business.

69-Research Services

Academics usually have ideas but took the time to research them. Book writers in particular and publishers in general are always looking for researchers. A specialized and growing service. Advertise your service around universities and colleges.

70-Room & Boarding

If you have a large house and don't mind strangers trudging through, this is one way to supplement your income. There are people who would rather stay in a 'homely' environment rather than hotels. Just watch out who you are taking. Don't be blinded by their suave appearance. Some murderers, rapists and pedophiles possess the most impeccable credentials in town.

It is better you work through an agency that vets your would-be clients' background before risking them inside.

71-Baby Wear

Anything to do with newly born babies is hot. Supply everything from baby foods to cots. Disposable diapers are particularly in great demand by busy mothers.

72- Bricklaying & Concreting

Making of fence pillars, Cabs for yards and car packs. Including Block making and Screen/fancy Blocks to filling and decorating the external of balconies or for the use of balustrade in small and big houses.

73-Sanitary Towels

Another everyday item. Negotiate with a manufacturer and distribute to supermarkets.

74-Disposable Syringes

Today's world of AIDS pandemic makes disposable syringes a hot item. Literally zillions are used and thrown away every day of the week.

75-Fast Food Packaging

I know of someone who supplies the McDonalds's chain of restaurants with packaging paraphernalia. He is a billionaire several times over. The fact that these are disposable items makes it a reliable business to get into.

76-Disposable Cutlery

Disposable cutlers, cups and plates, make great business sense. Expose your services to caterers and you are in everyday items- which mean repeat business.

77-Supplying Raw Materials to Manufacturers

Research this very carefully. Identify several factories and supply them with the raw materials they require at good prices. If these factories produce an everyday item like cereals, then you are into big, big money.

Good luck and let me know how you get on in
whatever you chose to get into. GO FOR IT!

CHAPTER 6

THE SUCCESS HABIT

Release the Budding within You

Within you, there is tremendous potential waiting to be unleashed. You probably didn't know you have it; you have listened to 'experts' who told you that you could not do certain things, that you were not good enough, that you were not born that way, that you are not talented like so and so. Absolute humbug!

Every human being was created with certain capabilities. Granted, that some more than others. But everyone with a functioning brain can apply himself/herself to any task actually accomplish it. It is all a mental game. The human mind if tuned properly can be trained to do anything. All it takes is the fervent desire to achieve something in this world.

First, set yourself a goal or goals to achieve.

Next, research what it takes to achieve that goal. Learn from real experts.

Thirdly, stay focused on that goal. Dedicate yourself to that goal one hundred percent.

Fourthly, work hard but smart towards achieving that goal. Victory is within your grasp. That potential within you is yet to be unleashed. It is your most important primary resource. Use it.

May be you are destined to be one of the greatest scientists that ever lived – if only you did research and carry out certain experiments. May be you are meant to be a great writer – if only you dare to put some thoughts on paper. May be you are meant to be the greatest sports person of all time – if only you were more dedicated to sports. May be you are meant to be the best actor/actress Hollywood ever saw – if only you join the drama at school. May be you meant to be the next Pavarotti – if only you join the local choir. May be you are meant to out-achieve Pablo Picasso – if only you mess about with paintbrush. May be you are meant to be the next Mandela – if only you dare dream about serving humanity.

No matter what your goal is, set out to tap and unleash that potential within you, because you have set out to achieve your goal; you are so focused on it; you are dedicated of it; you are working hard towards it, you will ignite a certain powerful force within yourself that will propel you towards achieving that goal.

Utilize Your Situation Positively

Everywhere around you, there are circumstances waiting to be exploited. The first one is you yourself. You are the most valuable and potent asset at its maximum potential. Your eyes must see and not just look; your ears must listen not just hear; your brain must think not just understand and accept things.

Your family members are an important 'circumstance' around you. As family they should be able to offer advice, encouragement, love, protection and assistance without strings attached.

You are entitled to it. Your neighbors (try to be on friendly terms) are indispensable 'assets' that could be put to valuable use. Remember your neighbors are your most immediate '(non – blood)' relatives. Your local library is an important 'circumstance' through which you can access important information, hence knowledge.

The elder (who saw the sun before you) in your community, might be an important source of knowledge based on their own experience in life. Your friends and friends' friends are valuable circumstances that if properly and positively exploited, could enhance your own personal circumstances.

Your colleagues at work could be turned into a powerful tool as you widen your scope and knowledge about your field of interest.

The stranger sitting next to you on a train, bus, plane (just break the ice by simply saying, Hello), could be that very important contact you have been looking for to help you solve your most pressing problem.

The club/organization you belong to could be the primary for that product you have just invented. Your hairdresser could do more than just cut your hair; he/she might know someone who might help you get ahead in life.

Your former school/college mates might now be holding important positions in society and could prove useful in your hour of need, (seek them out first before you go to people you don't 'know). Your doctor might do more than give you a shoe for fine, (might offer useful advice to your child aspiring to be a physician.)

Exploit, exploit and exploit the circumstances around you, positively.

Make the Most of Your Possibilities

Your ability to think is a possibility. Maximize it. Think carefully about every situation you find yourself in before you make that important decision, think and consult first. Ask all the questions you need to ask. No one ever died from asking questions.

Try to avoid rushing to the doctor to be pumped with medicine because you woke up feeling rotten. Try doing some exercise or and drink a glass of hot lemon juice, it might cure you and save yourself a needle in the backside.

Before you rush to the 'experts' to seek whatever advice you need, try reading manuals on the relevant subject or ask a friend first. They mighty answer all your questions and save you a bundle and time. Long before you go anywhere near a used car dealer, first try the auctions. You might buy a better car cheaper from someone who has simply fallen on hard times.

That man / woman you have fallen desperately in love with and gotten so worked up about, might be the perfect partner from hell and well known to someone you know, if only you had asked. That career move you are making might turn out to be the worst mistake of your life, if only you had sought the advice of an ex-employee of that 'wonderful company. That investment that promises you more than quadruple your hard earned money in two days, might turn out to be a nightmare, if only you had first consulted with Mr. Common Sense – free of charge. Maximize your possibilities and be ahead of the game all the time.

Erect Bridges, Not Blockage

The biggest obstacle standing in your way is YOU. You have created the tallest obstacle who keeps saying, 'I can't do it.' It is YOU who keeps despising yourself by constantly reminding yourself that you are a 'nobody'. It is YOU who keeps telling yourself that there is no point in even trying. If you constantly look down upon YOU, is it any wonder that others follow your own bad example?

You are therefore, the biggest obstacle facing you. You are too negative; you are standing in the way of your progress. So the first thing to do today is fire YOU. Once you have gotten rid of your negative self, you can then reinvent yourself. Create another new and more positive you. Believe that the only other person better than YOU in this world, is yourself. Then you can look forward to better things in the future.

Start building bridges between yourself and success, by simply believing that you can do it. That you can succeed in whatever you set out to achieve. That the only person around qualified enough to do it, is yourself. Remember other people have more opinions about you – you have facts about you.

When others called Abraham Lincoln a failure that was their opinion of him. But the facts he knew about himself convinced him that he could rule a country. He became the President of USA.

When Winston Churchill's teachers called him a buffoon because he kept getting low marks, they removed all hope in him. But instead he constructed bridges to success. He went on to become Prime Minister of Great Britain and also penned books used at Oxford University today.

When you think negatively you kill everything creative in you, the ruminant will be failure. However, when you think positively you build bridges that inevitably lead to success. Persuade People So as to Win

Having a positive attitude about you can influence others favorably towards you. People like you and warm up to you quicker. Your positive attitude also enables them to let their guard down and interact with you freely.

When you meet people for the first time, the way you conduct yourself will judge you by the way you dress. Your body odor can also influence the way people think about you. They might actually make a decision based on that "aroma" you subject them to.

When you enter that office, most important person at that moment, is perhaps the shabbily dressed; not so important looking and face covered in wrinkles – secretary to the boss. Dare hurt her feelings and you will be permanently condemned to the status of 'the boss is very busy right now and can't see you; should you wish to see the boss again.

Mind the feelings of others. Hurt feelings are sometimes impossible to retract. When you offend someone, apologize immediately, unconditionally and reap mountains of benefits. You win an argument and influence your adversary by letting the facts to look foolish. Always address the facts, not the person. Long before you ask anyone for a favour, observe the protocols of politeness and courteousness first.

So you influence a secretary positively by being nice to them and acknowledging their power to let you see the boss or deny you the chance.

You positively influence a prospective employer by arriving early for the interview. Don't ask whether or not you have got the job at the end of the interview. Instead, thank him/her for the opportunity to be interviewed and mention that you be considered only if you are the right person for that position. This attitude already has influenced the interviewer your way.

Judges are human beings. They don't stop having feelings by simply donning black gowns and grey wings. So influence them positively. Sometimes by simply entering a plea of 'guilty' (if you are really guilty) and not wasting the court's time and money, might influence the judge to toss fortunes your way.

Years ago some gentlemen who had gone to a foreign town was caught speeding and summarily thrown in front of a judge. Before the judge could utter a word, he requested to make a statement. Permission granted, he laid it on real thick that people like him, should never go anywhere near wheels, as they were responsible for the carnage on the highways of that town, was remorsefully sorry, utterly disgusted by his dangerous driving and the judge should show no mercy in dishing out the most befitting and harsh punishment on his books to very a deserving offender. The judge was left with no alternative but to throw out the case and thanked him profusely for such exemplary conduct. You win an argument and influence your adversary by letting the facts do the job for you, not by you proving them wrong and making them look foolish.

In Your Life's Jungle, Deal with Lion and not Chimpanzee

In life, it is always tempting to opt for the easier way out. To cut corners as it were. To short-circuit the system and get what you want quickly without earning it and without much sweat either. To hurry to reach your destination with the risk of night, rather than the safety of day. I know of no better way to court trouble than this kind of attitude to life.

However, when you develop the culture of 'confronting a lion rather than a monkey'; then you set yourself standards of excellence. You prepare for a marathon to run a mere mile or you set out to earn a PhD rather than just chosen career. In your mind, not even the sky is the limit.

When you want something done quickly, you seek to see the chairman and CEO of a company – the decision maker. Not the Assistant Deputy Director whom will only give you the runaround. You climb from the top (in some incidences), not from the bottom.

If you need an inclination towards politics (and crazy enough), then go for the job around. Remember one Abraham Lincoln?

Dream big, not small. Remember one Harold Wilson?

Choose first class friends. Live in a first class neighborhood. Sleep in first class hotels, even if you occupy the smaller room – but not in the backyard of the city and risk the most precious possession you have - your life. Frequent top quality restaurants in town, even if you will run into influential people.

Because you are a big thinker, you always go for the very best life has to offer. By confronting a lion, you will always be able to sleep at night!

CHAPTER 7

DIVINE DIRECTION

Keep Away from Rabbit Holes!

There is a story about a dog and a rabbit. The dog was chasing the rabbit through a field when suddenly the rabbit darted down a convenient hole and disappeared. For a long time the dog patiently watched the hole where he had last seen his quarry, waiting for the rabbit to reappear. But the rabbit had egress through a dozen other holes and unseen by the dog escaped through one of them.

Are you, perhaps, confronted by some baffling situation, frustrated by its unproductiveness and hoping for a change? Are you facing chronic claims of failure, ineptitude and inability?

Where do such conditions come from? Who enforces them? Who makes past experience the gauge of your present or future accomplishments? Personal sense, claiming identity as you, is the culprit operating through ignorance and fear to make you its deputy.

But you need not stand helpless. There is a solution to the problem.

Human achievements are often limited by the tendency to focus though upon one particular phase of activity when opportunity for accomplishment may lie in another direction. Many people work within a very narrow framework of mental energy, one outlined mainly by their limited awareness of their potential and their consequent blindness to their possibilities. Because this is a wholly mental condition, it can be corrected by a change of thought. This understanding lifts self-imposed boundaries from thought and thereby from experience. It opens vistas of achieving that which God has provided impartially for all his children.

Unhampered views of limitless good are suggested in the divine command and promise to the patriarch Abraham "lift up now thine eyes and look from the place where thou art northwards and southwards and westwards: for all the land thou sees, thee will I give it to you and thy seed forever".

That promise is a valid to us today as when it was uttered, for men live and work in what even physical scientists say is an expanding universe. In the boundless universe of infinite mind the scope of opportunity and range of activity are unlimited.

Apparent restrictions of ability and opportunity result from the belief in matter and material circumstances as bestowals and with holders of good. Centuries of false education have mesmerized humanity into believing that circumstances or chance or some irresistible, predestined force called fate (mistakenly identified as God's will) has the power to enforce certain conditions for good or otherwise in human experience.

Men's lives are influenced by such lies of limitation, as surely as humanity was long restricted by the belief that the world was flat. This was never true, yet men were governed by it as certainly as if it had been. How true it is that achievement is determined so much by outward conditions as by restrictive thought – patterns of fear, ignorance and bigotry!

True Christianity runs counter to the whole sweep of mortal thinking, in that in its revelation of God that reveal man as spiritual being, which is the reflection of His Life and Love; We must give free breath to thought before calculating the results of principle, the effects of revelation truth. Sometimes in our rational thinking we limit the action of God to certain dimension of our limited sense.

We cannot free ourselves from the hampering dandy of finite beliefs through the violent operation of human will or the reasonless action. We can only grasp the truth, by knowing that God in His divine principle expresses Himself, His love and His power through His only begotten son Jesus. Spiritually, inspiration confers the breath of vision and strength of purpose necessary to reject the presumptions of casualty and accept the inestimable gauge of true individuality and capacity and their limitless, capacity and capability in God.

Committed Christians pray daily for a fuller recognition of God's divine presence in their lives and undertaking. Their growing spiritual insight inevitably increases their ability and widens their scope of action. Through the higher reach of spiritual understanding they see that their future is not at disposal of limited being but is established in God, the Creator of the Heaven and Earth. All true happiness and accomplishments come from Him, through Christ the approved advocator of mankind.

The basic premise of mortal thought is limitation. It watches what might look like an unproductive mental rabbit hole of limited opportunity, ability, time and progress. The course of such erroneous reasoning is determined by the shifting standard of the physical sense that conceives of substance. But these apparent limitations exist only in fancy, never in fact and the relinquishment of such concepts opens up unrestricted views of opportunity for greater achievement.

Thought and action are one. Spiritualized demonstrable in liberated action that inevitably takes form in vigorous, fruitful prosecute of worthwhile pursuits. Unselfishness and brotherly love permeate it.

Purity is its propulsion and success its outcome

This could be effectively demonstrated in the experience of a young Christian whose mistaken concept of success as monetary gain alone led him to throw the weight of endeavor and prayer on the mainly material acquirement. In effect, he attempted to use Christianity for the attainment of willful wants that would benefit him alone. He spent every lunch hour reading Bible and pondered on renowned writers' thoughts that he felt might further his personal goal of worldly success. But such self-pre-occupation resulted only in increasing frustration and continuing circumscription. God hears not the prayer of self-entwined interest but of unselfish, outgoing love that places universal good above merely material desires.

One day the Holy Spirit infiltrate upon the door of his thought." Divine love always has met and always will meet every human need." Not the human "I want" but the human need! Not for material things alone, as he had believed, but for love, more Christly love in his own heart, love that embraces. Quite suddenly he saw that the incalculable wealth of divine Love is forever flooding into heart, providing all the inspiration necessary for the maintenance of a full and rich life.

From that day his activities widened and deepened because their basis was spiritual, that universal love which includes both motive and reward. Opportunities for advancement kept pace with his increasing love for God and mankind; never again did he feel the pinch of lack. More importantly, never again was he tempted to work out from the standpoint of limitation, or personal sense, through involvement with selfish aims and unworthily ambitions.

Christ emphasized the importance of raising thought beyond the mundane material and its accompanying limitations. He knew and taught that man with renewed mind can do exploit for God. He said to the disciple, "Therefore I say unto you, Take no thought for your life, what ye shall eat, or what ye shall drink; nor yet for your body, what ye shall put on. Is not the life more than meat, and the body than raiment?

Behold the fowls of the air: for they sow not, neither do they reap, nor gather into barns; yet your heavenly Father feedeth them. Are ye not much better than they?"

In obedience to the Christ, let us lift our thought and vision from the unrewarding prospects of materiality to behold the limitless fields of spiritual opportunity and fruition. So shall we be freed from limitations and reap the boundless, ever-ripening harvest of the Father's eternal wealth, love and goodness.

Endeavour to Maturity

Who is a matured individual? 'He's a person of mature judgment' – One who shows a maturity of taste beyond his/her years.' Doubtless you would feel complimented to hear such remark about yourself.

Yes, maturity is a covered condition: it increases your prestige, your value as a citizen and you as a person. It does much to make life serene, constant and happy.

Maturity should come naturally with the years, but often it doesn't except in the physical sense. We have all met the person advanced in years who shows the emotional characteristics of childhood or adolescence.

Miss (Nameless), had a shed littered with past 'crazes' – hobbies with which she had spent time and money only to forsake them after a few months. To fit from interest to interest, never to pursue anything for long is a characteristic of childhood. It should not be found in an adult.

Mr. (Withheld), is an efficient person in his late forties who holds a responsible post. In some ways he is mature, but in the matter of his religion he has never moved from those beliefs which satisfied him as an adolescent.

Mr. (Hideout), a former executive, shows immaturity in his retirement. Like a spoilt child he refuses to do anything to amuse himself or to help others. He spends most of his money on cigarettes, regardless of the financial embarrassment of his children upon whom he has thrust himself and whose lives he dominates from his armchair. Such thoughtless selfishness and refusal to accept responsibilities may be tolerated in the young: with the old it is inexcusable. Immaturity is a common condition. We all recognize the man in middle life who expects his wife to 'mother' him as his views with the narrow intolerance of a teenager. With a view to increasing your own maturity, give careful thought to the following: Prejudice

It is easy to see that this word means judgment before all the facts are known. Many of us jump to hasty conclusions. It is a mark of maturity to withhold judgment until all the fact is known.

Prejudice is unfair to others and to yourself. It may mean others suffering an injustice; it may keep you from the truth.

Superstition

If you are mature, you will have no time for superstition. In fact, you enjoy 'knocking them for six.' You will walk under a ladder with a mischievous grin. Should you find that thirteen sit down for dinner, you are unperturbed. You recognize that those superstitions are a legacy of the past when ignorance and illogical thinking were rife. Knowledge in the same way frees your thinking from the fears and restrictions that superstitions would impose.

Ignorance

The mature person is ignorant of many things, but knows it. The immature person is ignorant of many things, but doesn't know it! The former is always seeking to extend his knowledge, detesting the one-track mind and the parochial outlook.

His bookshelves reveal wide interests. The mature person is informed about the past and hopeful of the future, appreciating that although the progress of mankind is slow, the overall picture is one of steady advance.

Fear

In acquiring maturity you seek to eradicate fear from your life. Rather than fearing your fellows, you show an interest in them. You try to understand why they do; the whole bent of your life is towards helping them. You have discovered that perfect love casts out fear.

As a mature person you have no fears about your health. Leading a temperate life, you will have good relationships with others, plus refusing to worry has brought you to a state of good health in which with confidence you will remain.

You do not fear for your future; you have taken what steps you can to provide for it. For the rest, you have sufficient confidence in yourself – and life – to know there is no cause for anxiety. You can face even death unafraid. You have faced the fact that is inevitable. Secondly, you are either convinced that death is the end, or it is the doorway to a new and exciting existence. In either event there is nothing to fear.

More positively, a mature person is generally found to possess the following qualities:

Tolerance

As a mature person you regard everyone as your brother or sister regardless of color, creed or status. You accept that there is more than one way of looking at every question; laying no claim to a monopoly of the truth. Your motto is 'live and let live!' You know that there are few evils which do not contain some good and that man quickly contaminates truth with error. Maturity keeps you from being over-confident, dogmatic, conceited or proud.

Consideration

When you have reached maturity of mind, you are not so preoccupied with yourself as to be regardless of the comfort and feelings of others. Maturity allows you to put yourself imaginatively in the place of others and react accordingly. You are big enough to do this.

Detachment

Maturity enables you to view a situation impartially and unselfishly. A mature attitude to life is like that of an adult at a children's party – happy in their happiness and willing to lose, to be overlooked, if it furthers the interests and happiness of others. Even with your own abilities, as a mature person you can assess them impartially. You don't allow prowess in any sphere to fly to your head; neither do you engage in mock modesty.

Constancy

A mature person is constant, reliable and master of their moods. Being mature, you possess powers of 'sticky ability' and are not deterred by difficulties. You are prepared to work for distant objectives, things which may not materialize for years.

Cheerfulness

A mature person keeps cheerful because they don't take themselves too seriously. A mature person can be reprimanded and not sulk and can lose with good grace. Above all, you will shun self-pity and take full responsibility for your actions and not look for scapegoats.

Absence of Negative Emotions

No one may be called mature if they bear grudges or allow hatred to fester within. Neither is a person if they indulge in jealousy, envy or meanness.

These are the characteristics you must develop if you make maturity your goal.

Mission after Mission

One of the secrets of happiness is to keep busy. To launch out upon one project after another, to be planning the next before the current one is finished – this is the path to satisfying living. Especially is the above true when we do things we really like doing. Perhaps you say; I like doing nothing'. The author does too, but you will agree that you have enjoyed greatest satisfaction when you have been busily occupied with some worthwhile project. See to it, then, that the greater part of your precious leisure is devoted to doing things, making things, achieving things.

It is normal and natural to be active and creative. During the long aeons of our primitive past, we filled our days with hunting or growing food, treating skins, making weapons or canoes, constructing huts, creating pottery or ornaments engaging in tribal dances and ceremonies, placating spirits, making love and fighting.

Many modern day needs are met with little effort. It is important therefore that we keep busy by finding worthwhile projects, activities which will make demands on the mind and body and challenge skill and ingenuity.

Remember, being busy doesn't destroy peace of mind – it creates it! Idleness and consequent boredom are the troublemakers. They give us time to smart under imagined grievances, chafe under emotionally – induced aches and pains, wallow in self-pity and droop in depression and despair.

'There's no way out of it', writes R.A. Jackson in his unusual and delightful little book How to like people, ' you must have a project going and work at it. To be a man, to have any balance at all, any fellow-feeling, to have something to think and something to say, you must be working on something.' That is good advice. Be sure to follow it. And as you do so, you'll experience the following benefits.

Your Mind Will Keep Alert

Your most treasured possession cannot deteriorate when it is kept busy grappling with project after project. Consider what is involved.

First, conceiving the idea, whether it's building a shed, making a swimming pool, raising money for a charity, improving your home, painting a picture, writing a book, spring-cleaning, learning a language or raising a prize chrysanthemum.

Second, the planning of the project: how long will it take, how to go about it, where to work, what materials to use, how much it will cost.

Third, the actual accomplishment of the project: wrestling with problems which arise, reading the necessary books, acquiring new skills, imposing your will on matters and making yourself competent if not perfect.

All these make demands on mental powers and help to improve their quality.

You See Things In Truer Perspective

Doing things you like doing is therapeutic in the extreme. You face life's problems so much more sanely and surely when you have plenty of recreational activity. Boring chores, heartbreaking duties, daily tasks, never seem quite so bad when you return to them after a spell on a satisfying project. You see then that woes and afflictions and duties are only a part of life.

There Is Spring As Well As Winter

What is more, keeping busy on a project helps you to recover from life's calamities. While hands and mind are busily employed, wounds heal. Time carries out its blessed therapy and self- pity is kept at bay. So next time life hurts you, turn to some absorbing project delay.

You Are Easier To Live With

The joys of creativity will shed a golden aura over your personality. You will be less irascible, better balanced, more fun-loving, more relaxed. Achievement and genuine effort will make you feel rightly proud of yourself and self-respect, as pointed out elsewhere, makes it easier to like others. A virtuous circle is initiated. And of course, your very achievements will also earn you respect.

Keeping busy with projects increases your zest for living: it will put a sparkle in your eye and a spring in your step. You'll always have something to talk about, something to hurry home to, and something to anticipate.

Another welcome by-product is increased self–confidence. You become a smiler and a winner. You fall in love with life. Examine your present way of living. Are you a project person? What are you working on now? What do you plan to do next? If you cannot give positive answers, get launched on some project with the minimum delay. Once you have tasted the joys of project-living, you will adopt it as a way of life and never depart from it.

Become Extra-Ordinary

'Hey, you! Get hold of this pack! And look sharp about it!' The tanned legionary slipped his heavy gear from powerful shoulders and hailed the passing civilian whose gaze seemed intent upon the horizon. Such an incident must have taken place often in the subject territories of Ancient Rome. You refused to carry the pack a thousand paces on pain of severe punishment. At the end of that distance, most victims dumped it down with a curse, if they could contrive to land it on the soldier's pet corn, they did!

Jesus of Nazareth, in an attempt to introduce a better spirit into human relationships, told his disciples to shock the tough infantrymen. Their packs were to be carried an extra mile (Matthew's Chapter 5, verse 41). This spirit of the extra mile is one well worth cultivating. It is one of the secrets of happy, therefore successful living: for what life can be called successful if it is not happy?

Here's how it works in the sphere of duty. A harassed mother with a shopping bag, toddler and push-chair is struggling to board a bus. The driver is not paid to jump on to the pavement and help her, but does so. The mother is grateful: the driver feels good. The monotony and drabness of the day has been transformed by one little act. For a moment the driver was a knight in shining Armor, thoughtful, patient and tender. The extra mile ennobles all who walk it.

The teacher is not paid to give extra tuition to the slow plodder; she isn't paid to produce a play after school hours; or take a party to Spain: but does these things. It invests her life with greater significance, improves relationships with her pupils and makes her feel she couldn't change her job for the entire world. There is no life which cannot be immeasurably enriched by this spirit. How about giving yourself a daily injection?

The Extra Mile of Service

All duty is transformed if you regard it as service to the community. But think now of voluntary work in your leisure time. Millions have never entertained the idea. They are entirely enslaved by self. They think only of their own comfort and enjoyment. They have never heard that 'It is a happier thing to serve than be served.'

You don't have to engage in this kind of service. You could refuse and still be a respectable citizen; it is, indeed, the extra mile. Yet thousand testify that every pace of that mile brings rich dividends. Like the quality of mercy, it is, twice blessed.

Besides the gratifying knowledge that you have helped others, service widens horizons. It frees from the domination of self. Petty aches, troubles and desires are forgotten when you grapple with another's problems. Service makes you a bigger person – more understanding, more sympathetic and much happier. In others words it makes you more successful in the art of living.

The Extra Mile of Consideration

Every day thousands suffer and weep because people are thoughtless. If you would live truly successfully, you must often walk this extra mile.

It will cost you time and trouble, even expense. But it will invest your personality with a golden aura and you'll stand head and shoulders above the thoughtless ones.

This thoughtfulness will take myriad forms. It may mean dropping a word of appreciation to a shop assistant who has been helpful or sending a few flowers to a lonely neighbour in hospital or dropping a Christmas card to a pensioner living in one room. It may lead you to give to window-cleaner a cup of tea or cheer the postman with a word of sympathy as he plods through the slush with your letters.

Captain Flacon Scott went the extra mile when, writing his last documents with numbed fingers as he waited for death, he penned a note to the wife of his colleague Dr. Wilson, telling of her husband's heroism.

Thoughtfulness will teach you how to reprimand or correct people without hurting them: for rest assured only if you have not hurt them will you have achieved anything.

The Extra of Gratitude

This old world is crying out for gratitude. Everyone likes to be thanked, to feel that what they have done is appreciated.

Are you grateful to friends for a pleasant evening or a delightful weekend? Then don't merely thank them when you leave. Go the extra mile and send them a note of thanks and perhaps a small gift.

Are you grateful to that surgeon whose skill saved you years of agony or embarrassment, your life even? Did you ever voice your thanks? Lots of people don't bother. They make a big mistake. They say either, 'She was only doing her job: she doesn't need my thanks, 'or ' I suppose everyone is gushing with gratitude and she must get stacks of grateful letters. She'll guess I'm grateful and won't need me to say so!'

Remember that doctors are human and their hearts glow when they're appreciated, as yours does. They'll do their work all the better in the future if you walk the extra mile of gratitude.

Ask yourself whether you could gladden a few hearts around you by showing gratitude. Did you ever thank your old teachers, or the teachers of your children? Did you ever thank, really thank, people like the postman, the dustman or the paper-boy? Ever dropped a note of thanks to a pilot or a ship's commander to whose skill you owe your life?

A good criterion for measuring your success in life is the number of people you have made happy. Here is a certain way of increasing that number.

The Extra Mile of Generosity

Because of innate selfishness, most of us find it easier to be mean than generous. If we can get rather than give, we feel we have scored. We love to strike a hard bargain, to sell something for which we have no use. We are gratified if we can sell for more than we gave. In consequence, generous deeds are so rare they provide topics for conversation.

But meanness is, in fact, short-sighted. In reality, we rob ourselves of a light heart and the satisfaction of knowing we have helped another.

"Give and it shall be given unto you, good measure, pressed down and running over.' Jesus was enunciating a fundamental law of life. The measure of our giving is the measures of or getting – in friendships, love, joy, even material blessings. The mean selfish life builds its own prison walls and passes sentence of solitary confinement.

Are you making a gift? Go the extra mile. Study the interests of the recipient; spend as much as you can afford to add a little more!

SELECTED BIBLIOGRAPHY

J. F. ODESOLA; 'POWER for EXPLOITS', Christ the Redeemer's Ministries P.M.B 1088, Ebute-Metta, Lagos Nigeria; 1997.

J. F. ODESOLA; 'RACING for EXCELLENCE'', Christ the Redeemer's Ministries P. M .B 1088, Ebute-Metta, Lagos Nigeria; 1998.

TOSIN MACAULEY 'POSSESSING THE LAND' One-Hour Book TM, Dallas, London, Lagos; 2003

JEFF LUCAS 'GIDEON POWER FROM WEAKNESS', Kingsway Publication, Eastbourne; 1999

THOMAS J. NEFF & JAMES M. CITRIN, 'LESSONS from THE TOP', Currency

Doubleday

CHRIS E KWAKPOVWE, OUR DAILY MANNA, Liberty Publishing House

Lagos Nigeria; 2004

KIRK, A, A NEW WORLD COMING, London, Marshall's, 1983

WINTER, R D & HAWTHORNE, S C (EDS.), PERSPECTIVES ON THE WORLD CHRISTIAN MOVEMENT: A READER, Carlisle, Paternoster Press, 1999.

JOURNALS:

MISSION STUDIES: JOURNAL OF THE INTERNATIONAL ASSOCIATION FOR MISSION STUDIES, Hamburg, Volume IX – 2, 18, 1992.

INTERNATIONAL BULLETIN:

INTERNATIONAL BULLETIN OF MISSIONARY RESEARCH, New Jersey, Volume

18, No. 3, July 1994.

AUTHOR'S CONNECTS

If you have been blessed by this message, you can also
contact: Pastor Johnson Funso Odesola @
Redeemed Christian Church of God Headquarters,
Ebute Mata, Lagos, Nigeria

Phone: +2348035361325; +2348074368534

Email:odesolajf@gmail.com; funsoodesola@yahoo.com
Follow me on Twitter: http://twitter.com/PastorJFOdesola
Friend me on Facebook: http://facebook.com/
PastorJFOdesola http://Youtube.com/ PastorJFOdesola
Follow me on Linkedin: http://ng,Linkedin.com/in/ PastorJFOdesola

Favorite me on Smashwords: http://www.
smashwords.com/profile/view/funsoodesola

Printed in the United States
By Bookmasters